FOOTBALL DREAMS

Remarkable Football Stories for Kids

How 13 Footballers Overcame Challenges and Became Legends

ages 9-12

EMILY JOHNSON

CONTENTS

INTRODUCTION

Football is by far one of the most popular sports in the world, with one half of the world's population interested in the game and more than one billion people playing it.

'The beautiful game', as it is nicknamed, has the power to unite millions of people from across the globe, regardless of race, nationality or social status, all because they love football. Its power doesn't stop there. Football has the ability to transform our lives and means so much more than scoring a goal or winning a match.

So why does football have such a deep impact on us? Its physical, mental and social benefits are of course clear, but somehow this sport drives the people who play it to become the best version of themselves.

In this collection of 13 true stories about famous footballers past and present, we discover how they overcame hardships to achieve incredible things, yet each of them began life as a child with a dream. They prove to us that while their knowledge and skills are essential for success, it is their attitude which attains it and sets them apart. Their extraordinary skills, resilience, and charisma have captured the hearts of millions. Their stories go beyond the field, reminding us of the power of passion, dedication, and the universal language of football.

HARRY KANE

Harry Kane was only eight years old when he suffered the biggest disappointment of his life so far. "The boy is chubby and not very athletic." Those were the words that led to young Harry being rejected by the Arsenal academy after just one season. A tough blow for anyone, but especially for a boy so young, yet this youngster went on to become one of the best strikers we have ever seen in world football.

He has captained England in the European and World Cup tournaments and he is Tottenham Hotspur's all-time highest goal scorer with a whopping 280 competitive goals!

So how did Harry go from academy rejection to England selection and become a football legend?

It all began on 28th July 1993 in Walthamstow, England, when Kim and Patrick Kane welcomed their second baby boy into the world and named him Harry. Harry grew up

in London with his brother, Charlie, and went to Chingford Foundation School. Coincidentally this was the same school that former England captain, David Beckham had attended. Harry was passionate about his PE lessons at school and his teachers could see that he was always very dedicated and driven to succeed. He loved playing football, and whenever he played at school he always put his whole heart into it and scored an abundance of goals. He was a dedicated team player, clearly more technically gifted than some of the others but yet he didn't expect to be treated differently. He wasn't selfish on the pitch and he never tried to hog the ball if a pass was the best move. It didn't take long before Harry was spotted while playing for his local club, Ridgeway Rovers, and this is what led to him joining the Arsenal academy when he was eight years old.

We all know that to have your childhood dream come true is a humongous deal, and Harry could hardly believe it was actually happening. He was about to follow in the golden footsteps of his lifelong hero, David Beckham. Sadly though, Harry's sweet taste of success only lasted for one season. No sooner had Harry started to live his dream, than he realised that his fairytale football future might be booted right off the pitch. Harry's dad was the one who delivered the unwelcome news to him: the Arsenal managers had decided to let Harry go.

Harry had been rejected. He had been rejected because he wasn't good enough, because he was too chubby and not

athletic. The bleak reality of what had happened hit Harry hard. Rejected, faulty, turned down, declined… Harry wasn't old enough to fully understand the feeling of rejection, and his dad tried hard not to show any signs of disappointment.

He just put his arm around Harry and said: "We go again, and work even harder. Let's see where it takes us." And so that's exactly what Harry did. It could have been so easy to feel worthless and give up, so easy to walk away and never look back, but Harry's positive mindset enabled him to turn failure into opportunity.

Harry openly admits today that he had a chip on his shoulder after such a tough blow from the Arsenal managers. But looking back, he describes their decision as "The best thing that ever happened to me because it gave me a drive that wasn't there before." Harry bounced back from feelings of self-doubt, and he took the rejection and turned it into a driving force to succeed. He kept working hard, and at the age of 11 went to Watford on trial. He relished playing there and he did extremely well. So well, in fact, that they offered him a contract. Then, while playing a match against Tottenham Hotspur, Harry scored a hat-trick for Watford, and Tottenham offered him a contract too, almost on the spot! It was a tough decision for Harry but Tottenham were the bigger club at the time, so he took their offer and signed.

Harry was a fairly shy boy at Tottenham Hotspur academy. He hadn't had his growth spurt yet and he didn't know much about the importance of nutrition for young sports athletes

either. He was certainly not the quickest or the most agile of players, but he had good technical ability, a strong understanding of the game and huge hunger for success. Fortunately, the coaches there saw that he had potential. Harry worked hard at his shooting and put in lots of extra work on the training ground, as he always had.

When he was about 15, things started to change. Harry had a long-awaited growth spurt, he suddenly became bigger than his peers, and a new, more confident Harry emerged. As he grew bigger and stronger, he also grew mentally, and he started to make his mark at the academy. Finally, Harry's hard work ethic paid off and they offered him a full-time under-18 scholarship which he signed with Tottenham on his 16th birthday - the best birthday present Harry could ever have hoped for!

It wasn't plain sailing for Harry after signing though. Despite Harry scoring an epic number of goals during the next season, his career there still took some time to take off. Tottenham kept sending him out on loan to play for lower-division clubs to gain experience. This is always a challenging thing for Premier League players to deal with as the teams they are loaned out to are not usually as high-profile as their own clubs and the conditions are not normally as favourable. Often it can knock a young player's confidence and they return after the loan with an injured ego and less self-belief. Harry was only 17 when he went out on loan for the first time to Leyton Orient. Nonetheless, he kept his same mentality of

hard work over talent, putting in lots of extra hours after training, working relentlessly on his shooting. His determination soon paid off as everyone began to see that Harry was a goal machine. He displayed confidence in shooting with both his right and left feet and was a dangerous opponent in any position. He often aimed for the corner of the net, the trait of a world-class striker. Harry was proving what he was made of and his hard work and attitude were leading him to some well-deserved recognition.

Had Harry's big break come? Was he about to be signed up for Spurs' first team? Not yet.

Harry's resilience was put to the test again when he had to pack his bags and go out on loan once more. This time he was sent to Millwall, notorious for its reputation as one of the toughest places to play because of the harsh, volatile fans and how they treat the footballers. Players were often subjected to a great deal of criticism and lots of jeering and booing during matches. Harry had to develop a thick skin as the fans did indeed give him a harsh time. Nevertheless, he eventually won them round through his dedicated work ethic and persistent striving. When the Young Player of the Year award was announced, it was 18-year-old Harry! He had shown them all that he could do it but the next question was - would he be called back to Tottenham after his success at Millwall?

He did return to Tottenham but Harry's ultimate step into the Premier League was still to be a lengthy process. After Millwall, he was loaned out for spells to Leicester in the Championship and then to Norwich.

He was excited about the latter because it was a Premier League team. Unfortunately, luck was not on his side though as only two matches into the season, Harry suffered an injury, fracturing his foot. He unfortunately needed surgery which put him out of action for three whole months. Again, Harry's positive attitude, hard work and perseverance ensured he had a success-ful recovery and he was able to put his football boots back on in record time.

The 2014-2015 season proved to be a winner for Harry's career as he became a regular starter in the Tottenham line-up under the manager Mauricio Pochettino. Harry was given his chance to shine and he gave it everything he had, scoring a mass of goals, as well as his first professional hat-trick. He was blowing apart opposition just like a hurri-Kane and he had cemented his place on the team!

Harry has been a player with unwavering confidence in his abilities, and his attitude throughout his career has been a large contributor to his success. He had to work tirelessly to get his scholarship, even harder to get his contract and harder still to get his shirt. Nothing was simply given to him. His sheer determination and endless effort have made him the legendary footballer and remarkable person that he is today. He has the drive to improve all the time. He always puts in extra work and never gives up.

In 2023, Harry was given the opportunity to explore new professional challenges and he took the tough decision to embrace it after 19 years of enormous success with Tottenham. On 12th August, Harry signed a €100 million transfer deal with German champions Bayern Munich. After experiencing a record-breaking start with his new team, he continues to this day to show his world-class talent both on and off the football pitch.

FACTS AND CAREER HIGHLIGHTS

- Harry has the reputation of being one of the best strikers in the world and is Tottenham's second-highest all-time top goal scorer. He is also England's second-highest all-time top goal scorer, and is the third-highest Premier League all-time top goal scorer. Since his move to Bayern Munich, he has become the most feared striker in the Bundesliga!

- Harry captained England at the 2018 World Cup and 2020 European Championships and has won the golden boot three times in his impressive career.

- Harry is a fan of many different sports, not just football. He's a huge fan of golf and he also loves playing cricket, tennis and American football. He's even been spotted playing Fortnite!

- As well as being a national football hero, Harry is a romantic and has a love story that not many other footballers can match! He married Katie Goodland, his childhood sweetheart. When they got married, Harry posted on social media, "Finally got to marry my best friend! I love you."

- Harry and Katie have four children, all under the age of seven. Their names are Ivy, Vivienne, Louis and Henry. They have two dogs, Brady and Wilson.

- They all currently live together in Munich.

I don't have time for hobbies. At the end of
the day, I treat my job as a hobby.
It's something I love doing.
DAVID BECKHAM

10

RAHEEM STERLING

It was the middle of May and it was pouring down with rain. Everyone was outside playing football in the puddles, splashing around, having the best time ever. That's what people do in Jamaica. When it rains, nobody stays inside under cover. They just go out and enjoy it, and four-year-old Raheem Sterling loved it.

Raheem played football all day long, kicking an empty juice carton or a tin can around because his family could not afford a football.

Raheem was running in the mud, pretending to be Ronaldinho, his hero. He ran as fast as the wind. He took after his mum, Nadine, who was an athlete. But as things go with mud, it's slippery even if you're fast, and it wasn't long before Raheem skidded and went flying into a power line pole. "Muma!" His cry of anguish echoed down the street.

But Muma didn't come.

Raheem knew she wouldn't come. She never came, but he always wanted her to, and somehow he thought that if he kept calling, maybe one day she would.

Raheem's friends heard a soft and concerned voice from down the road as they helped him to his feet.

"What have you done this time, Raheem?" His grandmother was hurrying along to see what had happened. The little boy had a grazed knee and a swollen lip.

"I want muma!" he cried.

"Come on, little one. Let's get you a grapenut ice-cream to make that swollen lip feel better," his grandma said, trying to distract her grandson with the thought of his favourite ice-cream. Raheem wanted the ice-cream, but more than anything he just wanted his mum to come.

Raheem's mum wasn't going to be coming anytime soon though. Raheem's father had died from a gunshot wound two years earlier and Nadine didn't have enough money to bring up Raheem and his step-sister, Lakima. They lived in poverty and she decided to work in England as a nurse and try to make a better life for her son and daughter. The two children stayed with their grandmother in Kingston, Jamaica, and Raheem used to watch his friends with their mums. He felt so jealous! He missed his mum so much sometimes that it hurt inside. He didn't really understand at the time what his mum was doing for him and his sister. He just knew that she had gone. His grandma was the best that he could have

wished for, but everybody wants their mum when they're little. Luckily when Raheem was five years old, Nadine took them to London to be with her.

Raheem let out the most enormous yawn. "I'm so tired. I want to go back to sleep," he said as he climbed on the bed that Nadine was changing. "Get off of there right now!" she scolded. Raheem sensed that his mum meant business and he climbed off. Nadine knew it was tough on her children. They had to get up at 5am every single morning before school. Whilst most children were tucked up cosy in bed until 7am, enjoying a nourishing break-fast at home, Raheem and his sister had to help clean the hotel that their mum worked at. "Come on, we only have a few more rooms left. Go and start the bathroom with your sister."

Raheem hated cleaning the toilet the most. There were days it was so smelly and dirty, and sometimes it hadn't even been flushed. "Disgusting!" He looked down the toilet and then up at his sister. "You have to do this one, Lakima!" But Raheem's sister was having none of it and she pulled Raheem by the ear. Raheem pushed her off and they started shouting at each other.

"OK, enough is enough! I will finish it today," said Nadine. "Go and choose your breakfast from the vending machine!" And that was the start of their day, each and every day before they went to school - a cleaning session and a sugary breakfast coughed up by a machine.

Raheem didn't do well at school. He simply wasn't interested in learning and he didn't really want to make any friends either.

Nowadays when Raheem reflects on his school days, he feels regret because he remembers being mischievous. He drove his mum crazy! It was a Thursday and Nadine had been called into the headteacher's office yet again.

"Mrs Sterling, your son simply doesn't want to listen. He can't even sit still. He's a tiny ball of energy, and sometimes this makes him angry and aggressive with other kids." Nadine listened, fearing the worst. "I don't know if this school is the right place for Raheem."

Nadine's fears were justified and Raheem was excluded from primary school. She knew that her son wasn't a great fan of school. He'd told her how he spent every lesson dreaming of break time when he could head outside to run around in the playground pretending to be Ronaldinho. Old habits die hard and football was all that he cared about. So Raheem was sent to a special unit where he had specialised attention. The saddest part for Raheem was always on the bus that used to pick him up and drop him off each day. He would look out of the window and see other boys and girls walking to school on their own, having a laugh. I just want to be like them. I want to do that. There's nothing wrong with me. I'm just quiet. I'm a normal boy.

Raheem wanted to get back to normality, back to his school and he set to work on his best behaviour as quickly as possible. Eventually he was allowed to leave the special unit and return to his mainstream school, and shortly after, he experienced a life-changing moment. He met a man named Clive Ellington. He used to mentor the children in his neighbourhood who didn't have their dads around. He genuinely cared about Raheem.

"What do you really love doing?" he asked Raheem one day.

"I love playing football!" Raheem replied, without hesitation.

Clive took a long look at Raheem. "Well, luck has it that I run a little Sunday League team. You should come and play with us one day." That conversation proved to be life-changing for Raheem, as from then on his life had focus and it was football all the way.

It was evident to all who saw Raheem play, that football came naturally to the small boy with the mop of tumbling dreadlocks. Everyone could see he had a talent for the game that went way beyond his years. Somehow though, Raheem passed under the scouting radar and he wasn't getting noticed. His mum had to work so many shifts that she didn't have time to take him to any of the junior clubs, but then one day he went to a summer camp that was run by Queens Park Rangers. A scout, John Crieth, recommended that 10-year-old Raheem be given a trial at the club.

"He's a bit small. He'll be eaten alive on the pitch," the coaches commented with each other, clearly unimpressed when Raheem stepped off the bus and walked across the grounds. He lacked height compared to the other players. John grinned knowingly.

"I'm telling you. Keep an eye on him and you'll see there's more to this kid than meets the eye."

Next, they were on the pitch and Raheem had the ball. The centreback was coming towards him and he was big. As he got closer he looked huge! He could leave me for dead. But Raheem ran as fast as lightning. He got two or three yards away from his opponent and knocked the ball past him. His speed and ball control were exceptional and his right foot hit the ball.

Goooooooooaaaaaaaal! He celebrated the victory with what has since become his world famous, iconic back-flip.

Play continued. True enough, the bullies on the pitch thought that they could intimidate him, but they couldn't even get close. Raheem was pelting down the wing ready to line up a good pass when he saw a tackle coming from the left. It was too late. A bruising tackle on the ankle. This one sent him flying and he came down hard. Ouch! His opponent gave him a hand up.

"You all right, mate?"

"No worries," Raheem nodded as he dusted himself down and got on with it. He wasn't bothered for an instant. It was all part of the game. He was fearless, he knew how to ride the tackles and never made a big deal about it. Soon it became obvious to all that this young boy from Jamaica had a significant advantage - he'd played street football. Queens Park Rangers knew they'd found a winner.

Raheem came off the pitch after the match and the coaches clapped enthusiastically. John gave him an affectionate pat on the head.

"Well done, lad. This is just the beginning."

Raheem was beaming from ear to ear. "Thanks!"

It was indeed just the beginning for Raheem Sterling. He went on to play for three of the best football clubs in England: Liverpool, Manchester City and Chelsea. Raheem Sterling is a truly remarkable athlete who has made a massive impact in the world of football. He has shown us all that to achieve your dreams you must have faith in your abilities, and believe in yourself. No matter where you come from or what your background is, you can achieve anything you set your mind to. Through hard work and determination, the impossible can become possible. From his humble beginnings in Jamaica to his rise as a star in the English Premier League, Raheem Sterling's journey is truly inspiring.

FACTS AND CAREER HIGHLIGHTS

- In 2012, Sterling became England's youngest ever player to feature in the UEFA European Championship, aged just 17 years and 342 days.

- In 2015, Sterling made a high-profile move to Manchester City for a reported fee of £49 million, making him the most expensive English player at the time.

- Sterling won the PFA Young Player of the Year award in 2019 for his outstanding performances during Manchester City's record-breaking title-winning season.

- Known for his lightning-fast pace, Sterling has consistently been one of the quickest players in the world. He can reach speeds of up to 35 kilometres per hour on the pitch!

- Raheem is a keen chef and spends a lot of time mastering his cooking skills. His favourite dishes include Jamaican classics like jerk chicken, or curried goat with rice. He said that one day his mum complained about his cooking and he used the criticism as inspiration to improve!

- Raheem has also worked with the police, as well as different charities and groups trying to stop young people pursuing a life of crime.

- Raheem is well known for being honest, loyal and kind. He's a hard-working player who has also spoken out against racism and inequality, and helped inspire a new generation of footballers and football fans who are keen to help improve the sport.

 I learned all about life with a ball at my feet.
RONALDINHO.

JACK RUTTER

It was a Saturday afternoon and four-year-old Jack was running around the house like a hurricane, full of energy as he always was. He flicked on the television and saw that there was a football match in full swing. Jack's eyes lit up as he saw the fans and the enthusiasm oozing out of the screen before him. Manchester United were playing and they were four goals up at the time so the little boy decided he wanted them to win - it was a safe bet! Jack's eyes darted all over the screen in expectation but one player particularly caught little Jack's eye, and that was Eric Cantona. He was so strong, quick, and skilful with the ball - he stood out a mile.

Cantona scored a goal, the crowd went into uproar and the French footballer stood lapping up the attention from the fans. From that very moment, Jack was hooked. He went into the kitchen and shouted excitedly, "Mum, I know what I want

to be when I grow up. I want to be a professional footballer!"

That same Christmas, Jack told his mum that he wanted a football. He ran downstairs to the tree on Christmas morning and started to rummage through the parcels excitedly. Why isn't there a round one? Where's the football? Jack knelt down and picked up his first gift. It was a big, rectangular-shaped box. He ripped off the wrapping paper and saw that there was a lid. As he lifted it, his eyes nearly popped out of his head.

"You got me it! You really got me my very own football!"

Jack's mum smiled. "Well, I had to trick you by putting it inside a box or it would have ruined the surprise."

Jack went running around the living room, dribbling with the ball. "I'm going to be a footballer! I'm going to be a footballer!"

The contents of that rectangular-shaped box changed Jack's life forever. For the next few years, Jack hardly ever put his football down. He would watch a match, see Beckham bend a kick in and then he would go out in the garden to master the skills that he had seen. Jack simply loved playing. Having come from a very sporty family he had inherited natural talent but Jack's path to success came from more than that. Instead of playing video games like many boys of his age did, he opted for playing sport, learning and improving skills. He never gave up, he learned from failure and he spent hours practising, practising, practising.

Then it happened. Jack was only ten years old. As his parents explained the news, he felt goosebumps all over his body. Jack had been selected to play a six-week trial for Birmingham youth team. His chance to prove himself! And Jack did. He got signed after only three weeks of his trial.

Jack spent the next eight years working very hard. He trained twice a week and then again on Saturdays too. On Sundays he always had a match. It was a gruelling schedule with school work on top.

When he was 14, Jack signed a two-year contract with Birmingham and sat his GCSEs at 16. Then he started training full-time and playing against top players, from the best teams across the country. He was regularly going out to play against Manchester United, Liverpool, Chelsea, Aston Villa, Arsenal, all the greats. Jack turned 18 and life could not be better. He had already captained the youth team and he was about to sign a professional contract with Birmingham.

Jack's team had beat Watford in the final of the FA youth cup and the players had been given a well-deserved weekend off. Jack had gone home for the break and on Saturday night he went to a night-club with his friends. They were having a brilliant night with lots of laughs and banter, but it was late and Jack started to head home. Outside the club, he saw a footballer friend. Jack went over and patted him on the shoulder.

"Hey, how are you doing mate?" Jack asked.

"I'm good, thanks. I haven't seen you for ages! You OK?"

Jack nodded and smiled at his friend, "Yeah I'm great too thanks. I'm just about to sign with Birmingham. Things are looking good!"

Suddenly, Jack's beaming smile was replaced with an expression of pain. Then a blank look came across his eyes and he fell to the ground.

Jack fell, hitting his head on the kerb.

He woke up with bright lights all around him. Have I died and gone to heaven? Where am I? I'm in a bed but it's not mine. This isn't my bedroom. Is this a dream? Jack started to get nervous and suddenly he could hear what sounded like an alarm: beep, beep, beep. He looked to the side and saw monitors flashing. A lady in a white coat rushed to the side of his bed.

"Jack, can you hear me?" I'm in hospital. This lady must be a doctor. "You're in Bristol brain hospital, Jack. You've been here for two weeks." What? How? Why? "I'm going to bring your family in to see you."

Jack's mum, dad, brother and sister all stood at the side of the bed looking down at Jack. His sister was crying.

"What happened?" Jack asked. Jack's mum sighed and took her son's hand in hers.

"You were attacked, my love, and you received a severe blow to your head. You've fractured your skull in two places. The impact also damaged the nerve in your ear, and…" his mum had to take a deep breath and swallow hard, "sweetheart, your ear…you are deaf in your right ear. You've suffered bleeding and this has caused some damage to your brain. These are serious injuries, Jack and you're lucky to be alive." Jack's head was reeling and he couldn't believe what he was hearing. Brain damage? Deaf in one ear? But…how…how can I play football?

Jack had been in a coma in intensive care for two weeks. He had to stay in hospital for another week or two after that and when he was eventually allowed to go home, he left in a wheelchair. The weeks that followed were extremely challenging for Jack. His injuries had seriously affected his balance and coordination. He suffered from constant pain in his head and he always felt so tired.

Jack needed to spend a lot of time at home resting and recovering. He spent most of the day sleeping, which was lucky because when he was awake he lived a very dark reality. His brain injury had affected his speech and whenever he tried to talk, he mumbled a lot and couldn't remember the words that he needed to express himself. He couldn't concentrate or keep focus on anything, and sometimes Jack became so frustrated that he broke down in tears. He tried so hard to stay patient and overcome his difficulties but after 12 months he was told that his professional football career was over.

At 19, Jack took the heartbreaking decision to retire from professional football. Both Jack and his family went through a truly traumatic time. Jack felt depressed, useless and scared. What am I going to do without football? How am I going to earn money? I need to find something new to do. Jack went to university and failed miserably. His sadness deepened and he lost interest in everything and suffered from bad anxiety.

But then, light finally shone at the end of the tunnel. It was the beginning of 2012 and Jack discovered that he could play in Cerebral Palsy Football – a seven-a-side game played on a smaller pitch, open to those with neurological disorders such as traumatic brain injury. This was a huge game-changer for Jack and suddenly he found his direction in life again. His adversity became an unwavering form of motivation and drove him to train relentlessly on his recovery to play CP Football.

Jack had to work very hard on his coordination and balance. Every day without fail he dedicated his time to going through sequenced exercises. With every little bit of improvement that he saw, he felt a step closer to being able to rebuild his new life. His family supported him every step of the way and their love and understanding were vital in helping Jack through six whole years of recovery.

Jack started to play for the East Midlands cerebral palsy team and on the pitch one day, one of the boys came up to him and said, "You know there's a chance to play for England if you're good enough." Jack knew he wasn't back to the same level he was before the attack, but he was close and he hoped that it would be enough. He wanted to show the entire world what you can achieve if you work hard and he wouldn't give up until he qualified to play for his country.

It was Jack's first tournament playing for England and they were at the Intercontinental Championships in Barcelona.

They were playing against Spain after losing against Russia. Jack walked into the changing room and saw his Rutter 9 shirt hanging on the peg.

As he finished putting on his kit, the referee knocked on the dressing-room door. It was time. Jack quickly jumped to his feet and joined in with the high-fives with his team-mates before the match.

He felt a hand on his shoulder and it was one of the lads. "You've got this, Jack. You're back at the top, so now show us what you're made of!" Jack nodded.

Jack went on to play the match of his lifetime and scored a hat-trick against Spain. He was playing CP Football at the highest level and there was no stopping him now. He was part of the elite again and considered to be one of the best players in the world. Jack became an inspiration to us all and he proved to the world that whatever obstacles come our way, we can overcome them and achieve our goals. Everyone can learn from Jack's three mottos: you have to be resilient, step out of your comfort zone and you have to have a good, positive attitude. Why don't you see how far your positivity can take you?

FACTS AND CAREER HIGHLIGHTS

- Jack captained the England team in the European Championship in Portugal and two World Championships, one in England and another in Argentina.
- He also captained Great Britain in one of the biggest sporting events in the world, the Paralympic Games.
- His last tournament was the World Cup in Argentina 2017 where England made it through to semi-finals.
- Jack now coaches the England Under-21 development cerebral palsy team and he is also assistant coach to the senior team.
- He is a McDonald's Fun Football ambassador and works in primary schools helping children.
- Jack has his own company called Jack Rutter Skills School where he works with businesses, schools, universities and colleges helping to motivate others and inspire them to reach their full potential.

> I once cried because I had no shoes to play soccer, but one day, I met a man who had no feet.

ZINEDINE ZIDANE

DAVID BECKHAM

It was Christmas Eve and little David Beckham picked up one of the presents that had his name on it from underneath the Christmas tree. He knew it, he didn't even have to go through the ritual of feeling it, shaking it, playing the guessing game, because he knew. He was absolutely certain it would be a new Manchester United kit. He knew this because that's what it always was! Every year, David's dad bought him the new kit because he dreamed that one day, his son was going to become a professional footballer.

Luckily, David's dad, Ted, had a little boy who lived and breathed football from the moment he could walk. He always seemed to have a ball at his feet, and in a way that helped to make up for his shortfalls at school and his lack of friends - he felt he had purpose with football. Ted was hard on his son when he played, though. Countless times during their

free-kick practise, Ted would shout: "It still isn't good enough, David!" David always felt a lump in his throat as he kept trying to win his dad's approval whilst his mum watched with tears in her eyes from the park bench.

Sandra Beckham felt that her husband was too hard on David but Ted always argued that if he told their son how good he was, then he'd have nothing to work on. Ted's influence was largely responsible for creating the player we all know so well. He would oversee David's free-kick practice until late at night, rewarding him with a pat on the back and an extra 50p every time he hit an intended target. He would also kick the ball as high as he could for David to trap it to improve his control - the pass-and-move style we later saw was a Beckham-senior trademark.

In the tunnel, 21-year-old Beckham stood behind Eric Cantona and closed his eyes. He could hardly believe he was about to play against Wimbledon at their home ground.

"Let's do this, boys!" Cantona called out to his team-mates behind him.

Beckham looked ahead at Cantona, his role model, and thought about what an enormous influence this legend had been on him. Cantona was by far the best player that Beckham had ever played with. He was in awe of the way he trained, staying behind for hours after training to practise more. He was just as impressed with the way he played. In fact, the way Cantona was both on and off the pitch made Beckham look up to him. It actually felt like an honour to play alongside him. As Beckham stood awestruck by the thoughts of this Frenchman, little did he know that he was about to play the match that was going to mark the beginning of a new era in football and particularly in his own life.

Manchester United scored the first goal of the match, crafted by Cantona coming down the left wing. Then Denis Irwin came down on the right and saw the chance to take the score to 2-0, which he did heroically. Things were already looking good for the boys in red shirts, making a winning start for the defence of their title, and the fans' chant could be heard: 'Glory, glory, Man United…!' Beckham had his eye on Wimbledon's goalkeeper and saw that he was off his line. David was at the halfway line but he didn't doubt himself for a second. His foot struck the ball and he lobbed it to create one of the Premier League's most famous moments - England's most-loved goal to this day.

The press went crazy and could talk about nothing else. David Beckham had become a national football sensation.

"So can we agree that all those 50ps I paid you for hitting the crossbar in the park paid off?" asked Ted as he laid his newspaper on the dinner table the next night.

It had been a long day at work as usual for Ted. He always worked a seven-day week but he insisted on stopping off to buy his newspaper before driving home. He wouldn't have missed seeing a photograph of his son on front page news for anything in the world. Beckham and his sister were busy tucking into their favourite tea: fried eggs, chips and beans.

David looked up at his dad.

"Well, it's cost you a small fortune for sure, dad. But yeah, I think we can all agree it paid off big time!"

Ted pointed to the headline and read it out proudly: "The lad can play a bit!"

The epic goal had gone viral. Beckham had barely made a name for himself in the League before the goal, but with 'that' kick, he opened the door to the rest of his life. It was an 'impossible goal' and even Pelé had tried to do it. And so the legend of Beckham was born.

The phone was ringing. David jumped up from the sofa thinking that it might be his girlfriend Victoria calling.

"Hello?" he said. David nearly fell over when he heard the England manager on the other end of the line! He'd wanted to play for his country more than anything else and at first he thought it must be a prank. But the call was the real deal. David ran into the kitchen, arms in the air and yelled, "I'm going to play for England! Yes, I'm going to play for England!"

Next in line, destiny unfolded into the story of the 'other' kick: the one on the leg of Diego Simeone in England's World Cup game against Argentina in the 1998. The kick that earned Beckham a red card and got him sent off, taking the blame for England ultimately getting knocked out of the tournament and being sent home. He felt so much shame. He'd made such a big mistake and he felt like he needed to correct what he had done.

A few weeks had passed since the defeat and David still

wasn't eating or sleeping very well. The press had been viciously critical about him, and his fans hadn't shown much compassion either so he had tried to stay out of sight for a while. That evening, David decided to risk it and go out with Victoria. He parked his car and they walked down the street to the restaurant where they had a table booked.

"Hey loser!" David heard someone call from behind. Just keep on walking, you've ignored it before and you can do it again. "Hey loser!" There it was again, louder this time.

David looked at Victoria who had become tense. Come on, you've got this. Just ignore it. You've proved you're strong enough and you've handled much worse these past few weeks. Keep walking. Act like you haven't heard it.

Suddenly a tall man wearing a baseball cap was in front of the couple, right up close to David's face. David and Victoria tried to walk past this offensive stranger, who then spat right in David's face. Ugh! This can't be happening! David felt the spit hit bang in the middle of his forehead and it slowly dripped down into his left eye. David was so enraged but he wanted to keep Victoria safe and didn't want things to get worse.

"Come on Victoria, let's go back home." He quickly wiped the spit off his face with his coat sleeve and they turned back to walk towards his car to go home.

He was at an all-time low. Only one week earlier, he'd endured angry fans surrounding his car and shaking it while he was parked outside the training ground. Then there was the letter with a bullet that was sent to the Manchester United headquarters. How could he have gone from being nationally worshipped to nationally hated?

The story comes down to two very different kicks: there's 'that' kick: the stunning strike the 21-year-old David Beckham hit from the halfway line in Manchester United's opening game of the 1996-97 Premier League season. Then there's the 'other' kick: the one on the leg of Diego Simeone in England's game against Argentina in the 1998 World Cup that got Beckham sent off and ended up making him regret what he called 'a stupid mistake' for a very long time.

Two kicks that marked two moments, one a glorious high and the other, a painful low. Beckham's strength of character, positive mindset and his deter-mined attitude helped him to overcome what he now looks back on as one of the most challenging times of his life.

It wasn't too long before the 'other' kick was replaced by the 'other' match. England were playing Greece, this time to qualify for the World Cup 2002.

"Foul on Sheringham – free-kick. Will Beckham have another attempt at goal?" The tension could be heard in the commentator's voice. They'd already played two-and-a-half minutes of stoppage time and England were losing by two goals to one. Then it happened. "I don't believe it!" The words boomed out of every television screen across England. Beckham's last-minute free-kick sailed majestically into the top corner, a goal that raised the roof! "David Beckham scores the goal to take England all the way to the World Cup. Give that man a knighthood!"

And so David was back in England's good books again.

Beckham showed the world that rather than allowing setbacks to define him, he used them as stepping stones toward greater achievements. He didn't shy away from adversity, he embraced it, recognising it as a vital part of his development as both a footballer and a human being. He continually searched for ways to improve, always courageously tackling obstacles head-on, and he learned some invaluable lessons from his mistakes. So, with his strong sport ethic, growth mindset, generosity, and his love and devotion to his family, David is a highly inspirational person and a fabulous role model to any aspiring football stars today!

FACTS AND CAREER HIGHLIGHTS

- David Beckham was promoted to captain in 2000, holding onto the captain's armband for 59 times over 115 appearances for England, the fourth-highest amount in English footballing history.

- In 2003, David left Manchester United to join the Spanish football club Real Madrid and that very same year, he received an OBE.

- In 2007 he made a historic move to Major League soccer and signed with Los Angeles Galaxy making him the highest-earning sportsman in the US at the time.

- A lifelong ambition for David was to own his own football team. In 2018 this dream turned into reality when he became president of the Major League soccer club Inter Miami CF.

- David was, and still is, associated with many brands, including Adidas. He wore Adidas football boots throughout his professional career, most notably his signature boots, Adidas Predators.

- When the Olympics came to London in 2012, despite not being selected for the football squad, David carried the Olympic torch via speedboat as part of the spectacular opening ceremony.

- David has been an ambassador for UNICEF UK, the humanitarian and developmental aid for children charity since 2005. In 2015 he launched 7: The David Beckham

UNICEF Fund.

He also supports Malaria No More, the global initiative to end the disease and the #togetherband which raises funds for health education projects.

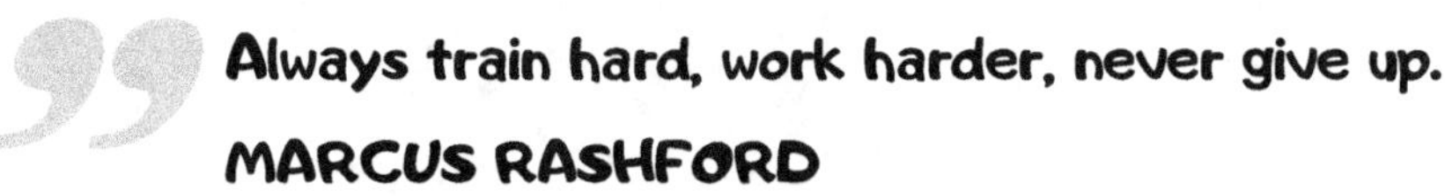

Always train hard, work harder, never give up.
MARCUS RASHFORD

40

ALIREZA BEIRANVAND

ooking around at the vast expanse of rolling hills and endless, blue skies, young Alireza tried to find comfort in the gentle sound of bleating sheep that he'd heard throughout his childhood in Iran. As much as he tried, he just couldn't find happiness in the nomadic lifestyle that his family had chosen to follow. They were a large family, Alireza was the eldest son so he had to work hard. They were always on the move, constantly trying to find richer pastures to graze their enormous flock. Alireza's heart yearned terribly for something more but his father was a man who believed in tradition. He was passionate about following the ways of their ancestors and saw only one path for his son - to shadow in his footsteps as a shepherd.

Alirez felt trapped. He yearned for so much more in his life than simply attending to the needs of a flock of sheep.

Whenever he found free time he played football and Dal Paran, a local game that involved throwing stones long distances. His father disapproved of both sports and even when his son spent time on his studies for school, his father was displeased. He had Alireza's future as a shepherd mapped out in his mind and therefore any other activity was simply a waste of time.

It had been a long day and both father and son were exhausted as they returned home after grazing the sheep one evening in spring. Alireza's mother was busy preparing the dinner with her five other children, and as Alireza and his father sat in the living room, a conversation unfolded between the two. Alireza's eyes sparkled as he talked about tales of football and his dreams of playing on a team one day, while his father's gaze held the weight of generations past. He spoke softly but firmly to his son, his words heavily laden with tradition and expectation.

"Son, our family has tended to the land and sheep for centuries. It is our duty to carry on this legacy," he said. Alireza listened intently, his heart torn between honouring his father's wishes and pursuing his own passion for football. As the fire crackled in the hearth, a silent understanding passed between them, yet Alireza felt unsettled.

That night in bed, the young boy tossed and turned as he battled with trying to build a bridge between tradition and modernity, between duty and desire. Alireza desperately wanted to make his father happy and proud of him but he also knew that if he was not true to himself, he would never

be fulfilled. He didn't know what to do…

When he was 12, young Alireza and his family uprooted from the confinements of the mountains and moved to a small town called Sarabias. Alireza's passion for football still burned brightly within him and he was excited to hear about the prospects of joining a local team. Despite his father's disapproval, Alireza went along for a trial and he was accepted. It was not long before he started to make a name for himself as a talented striker and he felt a new sense of belonging in this new chapter of his life. He could hardly wait for his first match when he would be able to prove what he was made of.

The chance came one evening in June. Alireza and his team were playing the semi-finals in a local tournament and his team found themselves in an unexpectedly intense match against their rivals.

As they ambled off at half-time, neither of the teams had yet managed to score. The second half began and the game continued as tough as ever. Alireza's team dominated the match by far with possession but the goals just weren't coming and it was almost impossible to get past the other team's defence. Alireza glanced up at the clock and saw that there were only three minutes left. The numbers on the scoreboard stared back at him dauntingly but determination burned in his eyes.

"Come on boys, we can still do this!" he rallied his team, his voice filled with resolution.

The opposing team's defence was still going strong, but Alireza refused to back down. With sheer grit and skill, he dribbled his way through defenders, dodging tackles and weaving his way past the half-way line. As he approached the goal, his heart was racing with anticipation.

"Pass it to me, Alireza!" shouted Babak from the left wing. Alireza saw an opening, and with a swift pass the ball soared towards Babak who with one powerful kick, sent the ball flying into the net. A goal that left everyone breathless just as the referee blew the whistle to signal the end of the match.

The crowd erupted into cheers as Alireza and Babak ran to their team-mates, embracing in celebration.

"We did it! We actually did it!" exclaimed Babak, tears of joy running down his face. Alireza looked at his team admiringly. "We're through to the final!"

The very next day, the team was warming up to play the final match of the tournament and destiny decided to take an unexpected turn as the goalkeeper got injured - it looked like a pulled hamstring.

With no time to spare, the coach turned to Alireza. "I need you to go into goal today. Are you up for it?" Alireza hesitated at first. I haven't trained enough in goal. I'm a striker! But I can't let my team down.

Alireza felt overwhelmed and was about to voice his concerns just as the coach added, "You can do this Alireza. I wouldn't be asking you to do it if I didn't think you could."

Alireza felt the weight of responsibility slowly diminish

and he felt a sense of determination wash over him. "All right, I'll step in," he said with conviction.

As the team stepped onto the field, Alireza took his place in front of the goal, ready to face whatever challenge came his way. The first half of the match was fairly straightforward for Alireza as his team put on a sterling defence and the ball hardly came near goal. They went into half-time with a score of 1-0 in their favour. But then the game started to get complicated and their rivals had a couple of near goals. The first hit the post and bounced off to the left wing and then there was a corner in favour of the other team which a striker sent pelting towards Alireza but he took a dive and saved it with both hands.

They were into the final minutes of the game and Babak was tackled by a midfielder. Their rivals had possession and the ball had been passed to their striker who was running like the wind towards goal. Time seemed to slow down as the striker sent the ball flying towards the net. With lightning reflexes, Alireza leaped and stretched his arm out, deflecting the ball just inches away from crossing the line. The crowd erupted into cheers as they witnessed the epic save and no sooner had the celebrations died down, the referee blew the whistle to signal the end of the match.

Amidst celebrations and euphoric team-mates, the coach approached the star of the match with a proud smile.

"Alireza," he said with admiration in his eyes, "you have a gift for playing in this position. You know you didn't simply save a goal today, right? You saved our entire season. From now on, I want you to be our goalkeeper."

Alireza looked at his team, including the injured goalkeeper who had watched the whole match. Every single boy there gave him their nod of approval and he felt a surge of pride and purpose fill his heart. The coach handed him a brand new kit and some gloves.

"You'll need these," he said. Alireza knew that this twist of fate had led him to discover a hidden talent within himself. But what he did not know was that it was one which would shape his future in ways he could have never imagined.

Alireza rushed home that night and as they sat around the table eating dinner, he excitedly told his family about the news. When he finished with his elaborate recount there was a deathly silence.

Alireza's father broke through it with the force of a sledgehammer.

"I don't like football, Alireza. You need to work and not waste your time on this ridiculous game." The infuriated man stood up and ripped his son's new kit and gloves into pieces, throwing them at his son.

That very night, Alireza decided to run away from home and he took a bus to Tehran. On the journey, he was lucky enough to meet a football coach, Hossein Feiz who managed a local team. He decided to help the boy and offered him a trial. Alireza jumped at the opportunity but he had to sleep on the floor outside the football club's door because he had no

money and nowhere to stay. On many mornings, Alireza woke up and found coins had been dropped on him because people thought that he was a beggar! At least the coins paid for him to have breakfast.

Alireza later moved to Tehran F.C. where he really began to shine and it wasn't long before he was selected for Iran's under-23s and became Naft's first-team goalkeeper. But it was the skill that he had acquired from his childhood game, Dal Paran, that finally made him famous across the globe in 2014. Throwing stones for several years enabled him to throw the ball much further than many other goalkeepers and news of his 70-metre assist against Tractor Sazi went around the world. Suddenly everyone knew about a goalkeeper from Iran called Alireza Beiranvand and shortly after he became Iran's first-team goalkeeper. He had fought his way onto the stage of world class football.

Alireza's story to the top in the world of international football is one that is truly hard to believe. Going from sleeping on the streets, cleaning the streets and preparing pizzas,

he is now living his dream as an international footballer. He suffered many difficulties to achieve his goals but he believes that it is thanks to those hardships he has become the person who he is today.

There is no pressure when you are making a dream come true.
NEYMAR

FACTS AND CAREER HIGHLIGHTS

- Alireza Beiranvand currently plays as a goalkeeper for Persepolis FC and the Iran national team.
- Beiranvand gained international recognition during the 2018 FIFA World Cup, where he made several crucial saves for Iran.
- Beiranvand holds the record for the most clean sheets in a single season of the Persian Gulf Pro League, with 21 clean sheets in the 2017-2018 season.
- He was named the AFC Asian Cup Best Goalkeeper in 2019 after helping Iran reach the semi-finals of the tournament.
- One of the biggest moments of his career was when he saved the penalty kick from Cristiano Ronaldo. No other goalkeeper to date had ever managed to save a penalty kick from the best player in the world.
- Alireza holds the Guinness World Record for the farthest throw of a football in a competitive match. He threw the ball 61 metres when playing for Iran in South Korea in 2016.
- In addition to his goalkeeping abilities, Beiranvand is known for his strong work ethic and dedication to improving his skills on and off the pitch. He has been praised for his leadership qualities and ability to inspire his teammates with his performances.
- Off the field, Beiranvand is actively involved in charity work and has used his platform to raise awareness about social issues in Iran.

50

ALEXIA PUTELLAS

It was 2021, and as Alexia stepped off the plane in Dubai with her team-mates and coaches, they were greeted by hundreds of fans. It was unbearably hot and Alexia was grateful to get inside the air-conditioned bus that stood waiting for them on the scorching tarmac. It was only a short ride to the hotel and Alexia would have loved to explore but she only had time to fit in a quick snack before she had to shower and get ready for the big night ahead.

As Alexia was driven into the city centre that evening, she tried to calm her nerves. The car pulled up at the kerb and she stepped out. Passers-by turned to look at Alexia, but she was too busy to notice as she stood and stared up at her image projected on the Burj Khalifa. She felt almost in awe of herself seeing her photograph lighting up the tallest building in the world. The image was as clear as if she formed a part of the

building itself and it could be seen across the whole city. Big, bold and bright, the gigantic projection showed the world that women have earned their place in the world of football and they are good at it! Wow! Her heart swelled with pride.

And now inside, as Alexia sat among the audience in the elegant interior, the whole room was buzzing with excitement. The presenter was speaking and she listened nervously. Alexia took a deep breath. I'm going to enjoy this moment. I'm going to stay calm. I want to look back on today and remember that I enjoyed every second. She listened as the prize-giving speech continued.

"What we've seen in these last years, is more women and girls stepping forward to play, coach, referee, volunteer, more fans filling our stadiums. There's no doubt there is more work to be done, however, we can reflect on this change with a huge amount of pride." Alexia knew that it was about to happen. "And now for the moment that we have all been waiting for…" the presenter paused for effect, "the Best Women's Player of the Year at the Globe Soccer Awards goes to…Alexia Putellas!"

The crowd erupted into applause and as Alexia stood up she felt that her legs were like jelly. She made her way to the stage to accept her award, cameras flashing, capturing the momentous occasion. As she lifted the trophy, Alexia's eyes glistened with tears of joy.

The cheers in the audience were punctuated by shouts of approval and the claps and whistles reverberated throughout the grand hall. "Congratulations, Alexia! You deserve it!" Her

team-mate, Jenni Hermoso hugged her, their laughter echoing in the vast room.

Alexia's pride was palpable as she addressed the crowd. "Thank you all so much. This award means everything to me." An overwhelming sense of accomplishment filled her as she gazed out at the sea of faces before her. Tonight was a testament to Alexia's dedication and resilience, a celebration of her perseverance and talent. And as she basked in the success, her very own victory and that of all women players across the world, she knew that this moment would last forever. It would always be etched in her memory as a symbol of the adversity that women had overcome to find their deserved place and recognition in football.

It had not always been a straight road to football for Alexia. Even though she came from a family of diehard Barcelona FC fans, football wasn't her first love because it wasn't something that girls really played that much. She started playing basketball, hockey and athletics, and her passion for football was more from a spectator's perspective. She started to acquire a taste for the game at primary school when it was all the rage to collect football cards, something that she developed a passion for. She swapped cards with her friends, intent on having the whole collection and she always saved her pocket money to buy a pack of cards on her way back from school each week. As her determination grew to collect the cards of her favourite players, so did her desire to play football. The game had captured Alexia's attention from all angles.

Alexia began attending a football summer camp run by none other than future Barcelona manager Xavi Hernandez and it was then that her dream was born. She later joined her first ever football club, Sabadell - the only youth team in Barcelona with a specific women and girls section at the time.

It was her second season at Sabadell and Alexia ran across the pitch, her feet gliding effortlessly over the lush green grass of the club's training ground. The sun beat down on her back, warming her skin as she dribbled the ball with breathtaking skill.

"Sabadell is lucky to have you, Alexia," Aitana, one of the older girls, shouted as she ran toward the young star in the making.

Alexia beamed from ear to ear, her eyes twinkling with determination. "We're all in this together, Aitana. As a team we can achieve anything we set our minds to." Suddenly, the coach blew a loud whistle, signalling the end of practise. The girls gathered around Alexia, their faces glowing with sweat and admiration.

"Great session today, girls!" Alexia exclaimed, reaching out to give her team the customary end-of-match high-fives. "Let's keep pushing ourselves, and we'll be unstoppable." As the team broke up to go to the changing rooms, Alexia felt an enormous surge of pride.

Despite the challenges she faced as the youngest captain in Sabadell's history, she knew that together, they could achieve remarkable things.

Alexia went on to make her senior debut at the age of

16 and then went on to join Barcelona in 2012. In her first season with the club she won her first ever league title. It was an unforgettable match from beginning to end. As Alexia and her team waited in the tunnel, the energy was electric. Their hearts were pounding in their chests and the anticipation mounted with each passing second. The distant chants coming from the fans, seeped through the walls, heightening the tension. "All right team," Alexia announced, "this is our moment. Let's show them what we're made of!" A chorus of determined affirmations filled the tunnel, then the mandatory high-fives and they were marching out onto the pitch. The referee blew the whistle and they were off. The stadium erupted into cheers as Alexia took the field, the ball at her feet. She ran fast down the right wing, weaving through defenders, her skilled footwork leaving fans awestruck. The crowd gasped as she dribbled past one, two, three players and then passed the ball to Melani Serrano. What an assist! Melani closed in on the goal and with a swift kick, she sent the ball soaring into the back of the net. The stadium erupted into screams and cheers.

It wasn't long before Athletic Bilbao scored and the pressure was back on, with the score 1-1. There was a lot at stake here and Barcelona needed another goal. Kenti Robles had the ball and she saw the golden opportunity. She dribbled past two defenders and it was now or never. Her foot hit the ball and it sailed past the goalkeeper, with the crowd roaring as the winning goal found the back of the net.

"We did it!" Kenti exclaimed, her voice filled with joy as her team-mates rushed to her, all hugging in celebration. As the final whistle blew, the stadium exploded into a sea of cheers and screams. Alexia's heart pounded with exhilaration as her team-mates lifted her into the air.

"Our captain is the best!" they chanted.

"WE are the best!" replied Alexia. They had just beaten Athletic Bilbao 2-1, clinching the league title for Barcelona.

Through all the excitement and celebrations, Alexia caught the eye of her coach, who gave her a nod of approval. She knew that the recognition of the victory laid on her shoulders, and her eyes filled with tears of pride. As they made their way towards the trophy presentation, Alexia realised that there was no feeling like it. She had overcome countless obstacles to get to this moment, and now here she was, a champion among champions.

Alexia Putellas has truly paved the way for women footballers, showing that they too have incredible talent, dedication, and passion for the sport. Her success on the field has inspired a new generation of female athletes to pursue their dreams and believe in themselves. With her leadership and determination, a promising future lies ahead for women's football, and Alexia Putellas is guiding the way.

FACTS AND CAREER HIGHLIGHTS

- Alexia made her debut for FC Barcelona in 2012 and has since become an integral part of the team's midfield, scoring a total of 184 goals!
- She won the Ballon d'Or for two consecutive years in 2021 and 2022.
- Alexia was the first Spanish player to win the prestigious award of Best Women's Player of the Year.
- Alexia played a key role in Spain's run-up to the quarter-finals of the 2019 FIFA Women's World Cup.
- Alexia has a strong social media presence and often shares updates about her life and career on Instagram.
- In her spare time she spends time with her dog, Nala Lamala, who she takes everywhere. She also enjoys playing the guitar.
- Off the pitch, she is involved in various charitable initiatives and works to promote women's football in Spain.

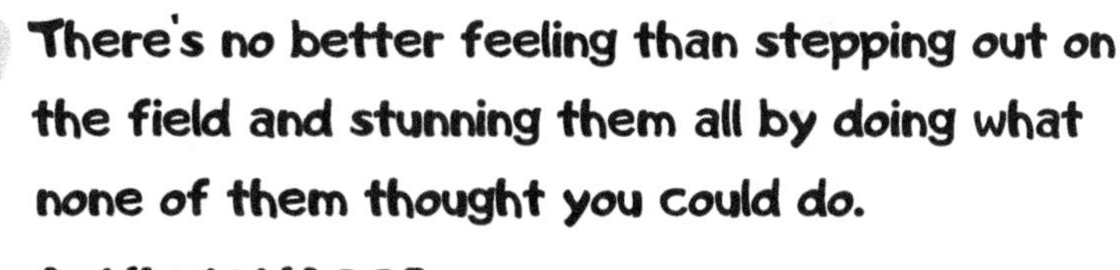

There's no better feeling than stepping out on the field and stunning them all by doing what none of them thought you could do.

ASHLYN HARRIS

CRISTIANO RONALDO

Cristiano Ronaldo was born on 5th February 1985 in Portugal where he grew up in a very humble home. Cristiano's mother worked tirelessly working as a cook and his father grappled with a job as a gardener and a drinking problem. Ronaldo was one of four children in a house with limited means and it was not the most stable of upbringings. Despite his outward bravado, he was a troubled and frustrated boy and deep down he yearned for stability, peace, and the chance to simply be a carefree child in the midst of their poverty-stricken reality. Frustration and anger often boiled within him and Cristiano had difficulty controlling his temper.

At school he was always in trouble for getting involved in conflicts and his parents had been called to the headteacher's office on numerous occasions. Poor Cristiano's mum would sit and listen time after time to the same old story: "Your son

is very hard-headed and he is reluctant to take advice from his teachers. He shows no enthusiasm at all for his studies and he is always causing problems with his peers."

Cristiano's mum always took a deep breath and promised: "My Cristiano will get better, he just lacks maturity."

But maturity had nothing to do with it. Cristiano didn't have any interest at all in his school subjects. The only activity that he was interested in from a very young age was football. That's all he ever wanted to do. He would skip meals at home to go out into the garden and play football, or sometimes even escape from his bedroom window to go and play while he was supposed to be doing homework.

One hot day in June, Ronaldo was in the middle of a history lesson and he was feeling tired. He felt like the school day was never going to end. This is so boring. I could honestly go to sleep here on my desk! Another boy, Mateo, came over to his table and picked up Ronaldo's pencil case. "That is mine. You stole it!" Mateo shouted. Ronaldo jumped up.

"Give that back to me, you rat! That's my pencil case!"

He ran at Mateo like a bull in a china shop, knocking him off of his feet and the two boys went rolling across the floor, pulling each other's hair. The teacher ran over to intervene, firmly reprimanding the boy for his behaviour. Fuming with anger and frustration, Ronaldo impulsively grabbed a chair and threw it at the teacher, hitting him hard in the knees.

Shock rippled through the classroom as the children witnessed their teacher on the floor, turning bright red in

anger. The teacher stood up visibly shaken and his voice was laden with rage.

"That is totally unacceptable behaviour! Go straight to the headteacher's office and wait outside!" Ronaldo didn't care. He was always sent to the headteacher's office for one reason or another so what difference did it make? Sadly, he didn't know at the time, but this would be the last time he would be sent to see the head. In fact it would be the last time that he ever set foot inside that school because the consequences of his actions had been set in motion. Ronaldo was expelled, changing the course of his academic journey forever.

Cristiano's parents were very disappointed. But the boy himself, although he showed some remorse for causing his parents distress, wasn't ashamed to have been kicked out. He went through the motions in another school for a while but he realised that his obsession was football and he simply wanted to be able to play the game that he loved. When Cristiano was 15 he decided to leave school and practise full-time. And in 2001, Ronaldo joined Sporting CP in Madeira.

It looked like things were taking a turn for the better for Cristiano. He was out on the pitch with his team playing a practice match and he called over to his team-mate Luis for an assist.

"Just get the ball into the box and keep it low. I'll do the rest." Luis nodded and did as Cristiano had suggested, passing the ball to Cristiano who pelted it into the bottom right corner. The goalkeeper came nowhere close. The two players high-fived and the coach congratulated them both on their tactics, calling the session to an end. As the boys walked off the pitch, Cristiano suddenly felt like a thousand butterflies were fluttering in chest, causing his heart to race uncontrollably. He placed a trembling hand on his chest, struggling to catch his breath.

"Are you OK?" asked the coach.

Ronaldo turned pale and looked worried as he replied "I keep getting this really strange feeling in my chest. It's like my heart has a life of its own and it starts beating like a wild animal is in there."

The coach looked concerned. "I think we should book you an appointment with the team doctor to get that checked."

The appointment was booked for the very next day and Cristiano had to undergo a series of tests to give his heart a full check-up.

Two days later he was called back to discuss the results. He entered the doctor's surgery with his anxious mother by his side and the doctor's grave expression sent waves of anxiety

through them both.

"Your son has a heart condition," the doctor said gently, his words cutting through the air like a knife. "The disorder is called tachycardia and if left untreated it can cause stroke or heart failure." The air suddenly felt so dense that Cristiano found it hard to breathe. He didn't know what to say. He was only 15 and it was a big blow for a boy his age, more so an athlete. His mother finally spoke.

"How can we cure it? What do we need to do?"

The doctor briefly paused before speaking with enormous compassion showing in his eyes. "Cristiano will need surgery. It's a very delicate procedure, but it offers the best chance for a long and healthy life ahead."

Tears welled up in Cristiano's mother's eyes as she clutched her son's hand tightly. "We'll do whatever it takes," she said with courage and conviction. She looked at Cristiano, smiling through her tears and said, "We're in this together, son. We'll do whatever it takes to get you fit and strong again." One week later, Ronaldo underwent heart surgery at the age of 15.

Luckily, Ronaldo's recovery was seamless and he was able to return to the field in record time with a determination to fight fit and fulfil his football dream. He trained with courage grabbing goals and headlines along the way and he began to make a name for himself showing his unwavering talent on the world stage of elite football.

At the age of 18, he signed with Manchester United, quickly finding his feet in the new club by winning the FA

Cup in his very first season. The entire world was left in awe of the Portuguese player as he went on to claim three consecutive Premier League titles, the Champions League and the FIFA World Cup. Cristiano Ronaldo was hailed as one of the greatest footballers of his generation and fans adored him.

It was not all plain sailing though. As he navigated the highs and lows of fame, fortune, and relentless scrutiny both on and off the pitch, he never lost sight of who he was at his core - a young man who simply loved playing the beautiful game. The problem was that Ronaldo still had trouble controlling his anger…

Manchester United were playing against Portsmouth and the score was 1-1. Tensions were running high and Ronaldo was chasing a defender on the right wing. He had a trick up his sleeve but the Portsmouth player Richard Hughes got in the way and there was a dispute over a foul. The referee blew the whistle and asked Hughes to clarify what had happened.

"It was Ronaldo's foul, not mine," he said.

The Portuguese player was fuming. "Shut up!" he shouted.

"I don't feel like it!" Hughes replied.

The Manchester United number 7 took a step towards Hughes and head-butted the Portsmouth player right in

the face. The fans were appalled at such foul play and they started to boo in unison. The referee held the dreaded red card in the air and Ronaldo walked off the pitch. The Premier League also banned him for two games. Ronaldo regretted the whole incident almost immediately and he knew that he had to get his anger under control or it could ruin his career. I have to stop and think before I act! His own advice echoed in his mind and he was quick to give an apology to the press: "I have made a personal promise to the manager, my team and myself. It will never happen again."

In 2009 the world of football was shaken to its core when Ronaldo became involved in what was later recorded as the most expensive association football transfer in history. He signed for Real Madrid for a staggering €94 million, playing in the team for nine whole years. He then left for Juventus where he played for three years before moving to Al Nassr where he still plays today.

Cristiano Ronaldo inspires people across the world with his journey from very humble beginnings to an international football icon. He always had heaps of natural talent but he has had to work hard and with determination to get to where he is today. Cristiano Ronaldo is one of the best footballers to have ever set foot on our planet and he is an inspiration to people across the world. As popular rumour has it, if your life ever depends on a penalty, ask Cristiano Ronaldo to take it!

FACTS AND CAREER HIGHLIGHTS

- Cristiano Ronaldo is the highest international goal scorer among active male football players, with a total of 118 goals scored for Portugal.
- Ronaldo has won four Ballon d'Or awards, four Champions League titles, two La Liga titles, and numerous other titles and awards.
- He won the Puskas Award, a prize given for the best scored goal in a calendar year. Cristiano Ronaldo was the first-ever winner of the award and he won it for his long-range goal against FC Porto in 2008-09.
- In September of 2021, in a match against West Ham, Ronaldo clocked the speed of 32.51 km/h to become the fastest football player to do so in any match.
- When Ronaldo jumps in a match, he generates five times the power of a cheetah in full flight.
- Ronaldo is a successful business man off of the football pitch. He has a line of CR7 branded products in clothing, footwear and fragrance.
- He also has a hotel, a museum and several restaurants in Portugal. His museum, Museu CR7, is dedicated to the life of career of the Portuguese footballer and it is filled with items belonging to Ronaldo.
- Cristiano Ronaldo was named after the former US President, Ronald Reagan.
- The Madeira International Airport was renamed in 2017

in honour of Cristiano Ronaldo.

In 2018, famous Canadian musician Drake, released a music album containing a song called Blue Tint. Ronaldo is mentioned in the lyrics.

Cristiano Ronaldo is a subject of study at the British Columbia Okanagan University in Canada. Students who choose the course study the life and career of the superstar.

Ronaldo is married to his wife, Georgina and he has five children, Cristiano Jr, twins Eva and Mateo, Alana and Bella. He currently lives in Saudi Arabia.

Before you can coach others you must learn to coach yourself.

JOHAN CRUYFF

68

FRANCK RIBÉRY

It was a cold evening in 1985. Two-year-old Franck Ribéry and his family were eager to get home. As they began their journey in the car, they started to talk about what they fancied for dinner.

"I want pizza!" Franck exclaimed with delight.

"Well, seeing as you have been such a good boy, I think we can make that happen," his mum answered cheerfully.

"I'm hungry!" said Franck.

His dad tried the usual distraction. "We're nearly home, son, not long now. Let's sing your favourite song in the meantime." So Franck and his family merrily sang along to 'Frere Jacques' on the winding road to their house. To an outsider, it looked like the perfect scene of a happy family returning home. Things can change so quickly…

It happened so suddenly that Franck's dad didn't have

time to react. The lorry came out of nowhere. Or maybe it was there all the time and he just hadn't seen it? He had both hands on the wheel but there was no escape and as looked ahead, it seemed like everything was happening in slow motion. They were heading directly towards a lorry and his son wasn't wearing his seat-belt.

Luckily the family survived the inevitable collision but Franck suffered some facial injuries and he needed more than 100 stitches on the wounds to his face. In time his lesions healed but he had to go through a painful recovery and was left with bad scarring on his face.

For the next four years, Franck was forced to grow up faster than his years. Some people can be cruel and insensitive when they see someone who looks different, and Franck certainly did look painfully different. He had two elongated scars down the right side of his face and another across his brows. Franck luckily found comfort in football, and at the age of six he started playing at his local youth club. He was so excited and couldn't wait for his first training session.

It was a cold winter's day and Franck wore his hoodie pulled up tight over his ears and face to take the edge off of the icy wind. He ran over to the football ground and signed in with the coach, who told him to run straight on the pitch and run through the practice drills with the other boys. Little Franck could hardly wait.

He ran onto the grass and started the drills, sailing though the lunges, high knees and frog jumps and then moving onto

zig-zag dribbling.

"OK lads, all over here please," the coach signalled with his hand and all the boys ran over. "That was a great start. A great session of strength training! Now let's get the winter jumpers off and we'll work on tactics." All the boys took their hoodies off and Franck proudly removed his own. He of course knew what the reaction would be. He'd seen it so many times before. He took his jumper off with precision and pausing for effect as he lowered the hood, revealing each centimetre of the thick, fibrous scars on his face.

He heard the boys sniggering and saw them pointing at him and whispering comments to each other. Then Leonard, a dark-haired boy came over to him.

"Hey, I didn't know Frankenstein played football!" The boys' laughter spread across the pitch like wildfire and every-one was staring at Franck. A lot of children in that same situation might have run off, cried, screamed, called them names too, but Franck just smiled.

"Well now you can see Frankenstein does play football, and he plays well!" he replied.

The other boys didn't really know what to say so they just shrugged their shoulders and play ensued. Franck played at the club for another seven years and his team-mates didn't make it easy for him. He was ridiculed for a long time but Franck never went into a corner and cried, he never hid away

and he never gave up.

Eventually he was accepted the way he was, in spite of his household nickname, 'Scarface.'

When he turned 13, Franck finally started to get noticed within the football world and he was asked to play for the French League 1 team, Lille. His mum and dad promised to take him out for a small celebratory dinner to mark the occasion. They never had much money to spare but they rallied together with the little earnings that they had and headed out to a cheap and cheerful café.

They ended up going quite late because Franck had stayed behind again after training to work on his dribbling. When they arrived at the café and went inside, it was jam-packed. A group of teenagers were sitting at a long table and they started to point at Franck. One of the boys looked over and nudged his friend beside him: "What is that? It looks like some kind of monster." Franck looked at his mum and dad. He always felt bad that they had to hear people making fun of their son. He knew that they suffered.

His mum stood up. "Come on, son. We can go to the pizza place instead." Franck gently pulled her arm to get her to sit back down. He looked at his mum and dad and smiled.

"Listen," he said, "these scars are part of me. This is me." Franck pointed at his scars with tears in his eyes. "This is who I am and I'm proud of it, you know? I'm happy with my face." Franck's mum and dad looked at each other across the table and no more words needed to be spoken.

With tears of pride in their eyes, they both knew that their son was much stronger than they could ever have imagined.

It's lucky that Franck was so resilient. He was bullied at school and classified as an academic disaster. He was laughed at on the street and his appearance was questioned almost everywhere that he went. But this teenage boy from France had an unstoppable drive.

After his first contract as a professional footballer with Lille, Franck went on to play with a few other French clubs and then to Turkey where he played for Galatasaray. Here he earned another nickname to add to his well-known 'Scarface' and he was christened 'Ferraribery' in recognition of his impressively fast acceleration with the ball at his feet. He was honoured with winning the UNFP Young Player of the Year award and was clearly claiming world football status.

On June 7th 2007, German giants Bayern Munich signed Franck Ribéry for a club-record €24 million deal. He was on the big stage! He immediately felt at home with the club and very quickly felt loved, making friends easily. Franck met fellow team player Arjen Robben at their first training session, and from the moment they went on the pitch together, they had a connection, laughing together as they practised passes and free kicks. During their first training session together, Robben praised Franck: "Nice one, Ribéry!"

Ribéry with his usual good humour replied cheekily, "There's more to me than just a pretty face!"

After training that day, they went for lunch together. They were interested to hear each other's life stories, and they knew from that moment on that they would be firm friends on and off the pitch.

Robben and Ribéry won everything together and the dynamic duo went on to earn a fusion of their two names: 'Robbery' - probably because they ran away with so many prizes together! In Franck's 12 years at Bayern, they won 24 titles, including eight Bundesliga titles, the UEFA Champions League and the FIFA World Cup, a glittering time for a football team that seemed unstoppable.

Ribéry finished his career by leaving Bayern Munich and going to play for the last two years with the Italian teams, Fiorentina and then Salernitana. He retired from professional football on 20th October 2022. Ribéry's success in world football serves as proof to us all that we are capable of over-coming enormous adversity and that we can rise above life's challenges, however devastating they may seem. He refused to be defined by his scars and instead chose to embrace them. Through sheer determination and unwavering belief in himself, he transformed his pain into power. We can all look up to Franck Ribéry and feel inspired way beyond the superficiality of physical appearances, and always remember to accept ourselves and others for who they truly are.

FACTS AND CAREER HIGHLIGHTS

- In 2013, Ribéry won the UEFA Best Player in Europe Award.
- His form for Bayern in the club's 2012–13 treble winning season saw him nominated alongside Lionel Messi and Cristiano Ronaldo on the three-man shortlist for the 2013 FIFA Ballon d'Or.
- Ribéry is a three-time winner of the French Player of the Year award and also won the German award of Footballer of the Year, becoming the first player to hold both honours.
- Ribéry's charitable work has also made him a beloved figure off the pitch. His commitment to giving back to the community and supporting various charitable organisations have endeared him to fans worldwide.
- He always likes to give his time to fans. He says that he believes life consists of small things and that is why he always gives time to someone when they stop him on the street. He says his mission is to make people happy.
- After converting to Islam he married his childhood sweetheart, Wahiba, with whom he has two children.
- He is currently in charge as a technical collaborator of the Italian club Salernitana, which was also his final club as a player.

LIONEL MESSI

Eleven-year-old Lionel Messi paced from one side of the room to the other, feeling the sweat trickling down the side of his face. Taking a deep breath, he wiped his cheeks with the back of his hand.

"There's no need to be nervous," said his dad. But Messi always felt anxious when he was waiting to see the doctor. Despite his nerves of steel during matches, the thought of needles made him feel as fragile as a house of cards. He just couldn't shake off the feeling of dread. The sound of a child screaming in one of the adjoining rooms only added to his anxiety.

When it was finally his turn to see the doctor, Messi walked into the room with a forced smile. The doctor, a huge football fan, tried to lighten the mood by cracking his usual jokes about penalties and free kicks. Messi managed a weak

chuckle but couldn't shake off his nerves. Doctor Schwartztein was the man who had been treating Messi's growth hormone deficiency for two and a half years. As an avid football fan, he would take the time in every appointment to listen to his patient's stories. He would find out how many goals the little number 10 had scored and how he had scored them. The connection between the two of them, combined with the doctor's experience with children, allowed him to understand Messi. The doctor knew that Messi was all about football, but he also listened patiently, empathising about the bullying he received. Other children were very cruel to Messi for being so small.

Lionel Messi had been diagnosed with a hormone growth disease since birth, which affected his physical development and the prospects of his future career. While most kids were busy growing taller, Lionel struggled with his height, and for the first 11 years of his life particularly, his lack of height had made him an easy target for teasing on the football field and at school. But little Messi was a mini football prodigy with dreams as big as his rivals' egos and he was a vital part of the Newell's team. Aged 11, he was already dribbling circles around his peers, but they couldn't see past his size to recognise his talent.

While other kids were going through their growth spurts, Lionel remained short and skinny, earning him the unfortunate nickname of 'Mini Messi' from the playground bullies. But his dad, a wise and caring man, saw beyond the taunts and

knew that his son was going to do wonderful things one day.

It was the night before a big Newell's match, and Messi was dreading all the teasing and sniggering that he would have to endure the following day. Messi was in his pyjamas and his dad had come into his bedroom to say goodnight.

"Dad, why do they always make fun of me?" the young boy asked, flicking through his favourite football magazine.

His father smiled knowingly and replied, "They're just jealous, son. They see your potential and it scares them. You're a threat to them."

Messi took a deep breath and hoped that one day he would understand what his dad was saying. "Goodnight, dad," he whispered.

"Goodnight my *campeón*," his dad replied.

The next day they had an early start at the club grounds. Newell's players were called out to get ready for the match but Messi had been left on the bench. It wasn't long before the team were losing badly and Messi's grandma, his greatest fan, shouted at the coach. "Put him on!"

The manager looked unsure and the grandma shouted crossly this time: "Put the boy on!" So the coach obediently did as he was told.

Young Messi stepped out onto the pitch with his shirt that looked two sizes too big, but everyone could see the determination in his eyes. The opposing team began to laugh at his small stature.

"Hey, dwarf. Where's Snow White?" Another team

underestimating his abilities. As the game evolved, Messi showcased his incredible skill and speed on the pitch, dribbling past defenders twice his size.

Despite the taunts and jeers from the other team, he fought back tears and focused on the game, hearing his father's words from breakfast that morning echoing in his mind. "Believe in yourself, Lio. You are destined for greatness."

With minutes left on the clock and the score tied, Messi found himself facing the goalkeeper one-on-one. The crowd fell silent as he took a deep breath, channelling all his determination and passion into one final kick. Come on, I can do this! The ball soared through the air, past the outstretched arms of the goalkeeper, and into the back of the net - a winning goal that won him more than just the long-awaited approval of his team-mates.

As Messi celebrated with his team, the once-mocking opponents now stood in awe of 'the dwarf' who had proven them all wrong.

Now there was no mention of Snow White! With a smile on his face and a fire in his heart, Messi knew that this was just the beginning of his incredible journey to becoming one of the greatest footballers of all time. He could feel it. He believed in himself and he knew that now there was no holding him back.

Messi continued to train tirelessly, working on his skills

with a determination beyond his years. He may have been small in stature, but his heart was as mighty as a lion's. Everything was coming together for the young footballer as Messi was also finally starting to see progress with his hormone treatment – he was growing taller! He was thrilled at the prospect of no longer being the shortest player on the field. But just as things were looking up, a terrible twist of fate hit Argentina and an economic crisis struck, causing havoc and enormous distress across the country.

The insurance company that had been funding Messi's treatment suddenly announced they could no longer afford to continue covering the costs. Messi was devastated. How will I ever reach my full potential now? Will Newell's still want me? Will I be small forever? Messi dreaded the prospect of always having to look up to his towering opponents on the field.

Parallel to the crisis in Argentina's economy, something more promising was happening in far away Spain. The sporting directors of FC Barcelona had seen videos of Messi and they recognised his immense talent and potential. Barcelona made the decision to cover the costs of Messi's expensive hormone treatment, which involved daily injections to help stimulate his growth. The club believed in Messi's abilities and were willing to invest in his future, knowing that he could become a star player for their first team. They sent him an offer, with the condition that Messi would be willing to move to start a new life in Spain. Messi and his family didn't doubt their answer for a second.

As the FC Barcelona directors stood waiting at Barcelona airport for Messi's arrival, they spotted a small, skinny, silhouette strolling through passport control. They quickly realised that what they had seen on video contrasted with their first impressions of Messi in person. They knew that he had been seen by a hormone specialist in Argentina. They knew that he had growth issues and that a club willing to sign him would have to pay for his expensive growth hormone treatment. But when they saw Messi for the first time at the airport that day, they thought they had made a mistake.

Messi could hear them muttering to each other as they walked to the car. "We've been conned. This small child can't play football. He's tiny. Thin as a rake! They're going to break this kid's legs on the pitch." For a moment, Messi thought they might send him back to Argentina. But he was not sent back to his homeland, and with those words echoing in his mind, he continued to train vigorously, working on his skills, persevering with unwavering determination, consistently driving towards his goals.

Messi continued with his hormone treatment which consisted of an intravenous medicine that he had to inject into his leg himself every single day. He never complained, never tired, never gave up, and by the end of the treatment he was 1.70 metres tall. It was not long before everyone realised that Barcelona's decision to fund Messi's treatment had not only been a success in the world of medicine but also a historical success for Barcelona. He was a vital element in creating a legendary decade for the club winning a club-record 34 trophies!

Messi's story is one of talent, determination and relentless pursuit of excellence. He went on to become widely acknowledged as one of the game's true legends and quite possibly the best player in history. He proved that the initial disadvantage of his diminutive size was in fact his greatest advantage as it allowed him to change direction quickly and play in any position. Messi's perseverance and hunger for football fuelled his motivation, turning obstacles into encouragement and trials into inspiration. His drive to do the best made him unstoppable and what Lionel Messi is today - an example to follow.

FACTS AND CAREER HIGHLIGHTS

- Messi won the FIFA World Cup Golden Ball and a record six Ballon d'Or awards!

- He has scored a total of over 700 career goals for Barcelona and Argentina and he currently holds the record for most goals scored in a calendar year with a whopping 91 goals in 2012!

- During his time with FC Barcelona he helped them win numerous La Liga titles, Copa del Rey trophies, and UEFA Champions League titles.

- Messi's World Cup celebration post from 2022 is the most liked picture ever on Instagram with over 75.6 million likes! He is also the second most followed athlete in the world with over 481 million followers!

- After scoring a goal, Messi points his finger to the sky as a celebration. The gesture is in honour of his late grandmother who always encouraged him to play football as a child.

- Messi has an extensive luxury car collection in his garage. His most expensive is a Ferrari 335 S Spider Scaglietti worth over $36 million!

Every disadvantage has got its advantage.
JOHAN CRUYFF

86

SADIO MANÉ

The scene in Madrid was one of sheer happiness and pure delight. As Liverpool's fans celebrated in the stands, what really stood out was the mass of people on the Wanda Metropolitano pitch. Their players were getting their own party started, bear-hugging each other and all celebrating their victory. And there, in the midst of the euphoria, stood Sadio Mané, a medal round his neck, a smile as wide as the River Mersey. There he stood with his team, winners of the biggest prize in club football - The Champions League title.

Sadio's story starts a long way from the Spanish capital, in the remote village of Bambali, Senegal. From the early age of two years old, Sadio was always kicking something along. If he could find a ball, all the better, but he often made do with a grapefruit. He was forever on the roads, just playing in the dust. As Sadio grew older, it became clear that his life

was not privileged.

His father died when he was only seven years old and he felt that he needed to help his mother, which was a tough feat for a child so young.

He had to work hard as a young boy and every day after school he went to the fields to work on a farm and cultivate the land.

He laboured away relentlessly under the scorching sun, ploughing the land alongside other children from his village. In spite of his demanding situation, he always tried to lighten the mood and make his friends laugh.

"Come on Sadio, tell us the story about the ostrich again!"

Sadio looked at them and smiled, wiping the sweat from his brow. "I've told you that one a hundred times! Let's get this job done and play some football instead."

The boys finished their work and went to get the customary grapefruit that they used as a ball.

When Sadio was 15, he heard about a football trial in Dakar. This could be my ticket to a better future. He was living with his Uncle Ibrahim at the time and he decided to speak to him about it. He ran up to his uncle excitedly.

"There are lots of boys going to a football trial in Dakar. Do you think we could go?"

Sadio prayed with all his heart that his uncle would agree. He was already beginning to imagine himself living the life of his football heroes. His uncle, a kind man who had always backed Sadio's football passion all the way, replied, "We must go, Sadio. The journey is long but I know that this is your destiny."

And so Sadio and his uncle undertook a challenging 500-mile journey to Dakar.

When they arrived, there were lots of boys being tested and getting organised into teams. Sadio looked around and saw that there was an older man looking at him in a strange way. He was staring at him as if he was in the wrong place. The man walked over to him.

"Are you here for the test?" he inquired. Sadio smiled and nodded. "With those boots?" the man continued. Sadio looked down at his battered and torn boots. They were in bad shape and extremely old. "And with those shorts? You don't even have proper football shorts?" the man carried on.

Sadio couldn't believe how badly this was going and replied weakly, "I'm sorry, sir, but these are the best that I have. Please let me play."

The man took a long look at Sadio. "OK, kid, get on the pitch and let's see what you can do."

Sadio went on the field to start playing with the other boys and when he glanced over at the man he could see the surprise on his face. Sadio showed his ability to excel in multiple positions and he tirelessly practised dribbling, tackling,

passing, and striking goals with passionate determination. When Sadio came off the pitch, the man came over to him and spoke enthusiastically. "I'm picking you straight away. You'll play in my team."

And so, after those trials, Sadio went to join the Generation Foot academy and trained with some of the most talented young players in the country. With tears of joy in his eyes, he bid farewell to his village, knowing that this was just the beginning of an incredible journey ahead.

Sadio was homesick in Dakar. He was living with a family that he didn't even know and he missed his loved ones terribly. But he knew that if he wanted to make it in football, he had to keep going, he couldn't give up. He trained relentlessly, kept his focus on football and believed in himself. It wasn't long before he moved onto Metz in France and then to Salzburg, Austria, where he really started to make a name for himself. It was his second match playing for the team and Sadio was eager to prove himself but their opponents in Austria Wien were tough and they had a strong defence.

The referee blew the whistle, marking the start of the match and Sadio could feel the tension in every bone in his body. Despite his nerves, he remained focused and determined. He had the ball at his feet and he was dribbling as fast as lightning, passing defenders effortlessly. He waited patiently as he saw another attack developing past the midfield. He held his position around the penalty spot and there could only be one outcome.

Goooooooooaaaaaaaaall! He skidded on his knees to be buried in his team's celebratory bear hugs. "Way to go, Sadio!" They all looked at their team-mate with pride.

As the game continued to unfold, Sadio's skill and determination were palpable across the whole stadium. With lightning speed he crafted the game and had the ball at his feet yet again. He darted around, closing down defenders and surging forward. He sprinted into the box, moved around to confuse his marker and saw his moment again. As the inside of his foot touched the ball, he knew it was a winner and he saw it go flying into the far corner of the net. His team-mates were all around him again. "You're unstoppable, Sadio! You're a legend!"

The energy on the field was electric, and Sadio could feel the elation of his victory pulsating through his veins. The crowd were still cheering relentlessly after witnessing such an elevated level of football and the fans were in awe with the Senegalese player's incredible talent and determination. His performance inspired his team-mates to raise their game too, going on to secure a memorable 3-0 victory, but more importantly earning him respect and admiration from fans around the world.

The match marked the beginning of a remarkable journey for Sadio Mané, showcasing his potential to become one of the greatest footballers of his generation. It was a moment that proved that with dedication, skill, and perseverance, anything is possible in the world of sports. Sadio went on to play for Southampton and then none less than one of the top teams in the world, Liverpool. But his biggest moment of pride came in 2019 when he was named African Footballer of the Year, a title given to him by his country, Senegal. Shortly after, he represented his country in the Africa Cup of Nations tournament.

Sadio Mané has always held his home country very close to his heart and he felt enormous pride as he stood listening to the national anthem on the day of the final against Egypt. But the match was tense and Sadio and his team found themselves with no goal by the end of the second half. They were going to penalties.

The team listened to the coach and then Sadio remembered the days when he tried to boost morale with his friends working on the farm. He gathered his team-mates and spoke with conviction.

"This is our moment. We have all worked relentlessly for

this opportunity and we deserve to win. Let's write our names in history today!"

Senegal stepped up to take the penalties with Sadio himself scoring the deciding goal with enviable, unwavering precision. The stadium erupted as Sadio Mané had scored the decisive goal for his team and for his country. Senegal had nailed a victorious 4-2 win! They had etched their names in history and become the architects of future generations to come, inspiring all with their incredible display of teamwork and resilience.

As Sadio and his team stood with the trophy, his words echoed through the stadium: "This trophy is the special one for me. This is the important one for me. I am happy for myself, my people, and all of my family."

FACTS AND CAREER HIGHLIGHTS

- Mané is known for his humility and his commitment to giving back to his community and helping others. He donated 300 Liverpool shirts to his village when the side reached the UEFA Champions League Final in 2018.

- Mané is not a stereotypical footballer. He says that he doesn't want a garage full of Ferraris and a cupboard full of expensive watches as he prefers to help people who are less fortunate. He prefers that people receive a little of what life has given him.

- With no hospital in his childhood village, Mané's father was unable to get the medical attention which he needed to save his life. In 2021, Mané built the first hospital in Bambali and two years later he built a school in his hometown.

- Mané also gives all people in a very poor Senegalese region €70 every month to contribute to their family's economy.

- Sadio Mané entered the Premier League record books on 16th May 2015, when his Southampton side faced Aston Villa and he scored three spectacular goals within two minutes and 56 seconds. This hat-trick still stands as the fastest hat-trick in Premier League history.

- In 2016, Liverpool signed Mane for a fee of £34 million, making him the most expensive African player in history at the time.

- After helping his country win the Africa Cup of Nations

for the first time in 2021, Mane was appointed a Grand Officer of the National Order of the Lion, highest order of Senegal, by the President of Senegal.

> It's not just about the money, it's about what you achieve on the pitch.
> **RONALDINHO**

96

LUKA MODRIĆ

It was an icy cold day in Zadar, Croatia, and six-year-old Luka was staying with his grandfather for a few days. They were sitting cosily in the living room for their customary reading session. Luka loved to sit close to his grandad while he read stories to him, losing himself in adventurous tales of knights and dragons. That evening, there was a delicious smell of his grandfather's famous venison stew wafting through the air and when they finished the story, they sat and ate it by the blazing fire.

"Can I go out with you in the mountains tomorrow?" asked Luka. His grandad tended sheep and goats and Luka always loved to help look after them. His grandad nodded enthusiastically.

"You can! And you can collect all of the eggs from the hens too." Luka beamed from ear to ear. He loved to spend

time with his grandad.

They both went to bed early as they had a lot planned for the next day and Luka fell fast asleep. It wasn't even close to sunrise when he was suddenly jolted awake. It was the all too familiar and deafening sound of exploding bombs from the well-advanced Croatian War of Independence. Luka could see the glow of fire through the curtain of his bedroom window and he felt fearful.

He went over to look outside and as he stood rooted to the spot, the most dismal scene unfolded before his eyes. The village below was a blur of chaos and destruction, smoke billowing up from the many houses on fire and people fleeing from their homes in desperation.

Suddenly, Luka's grandad was at his bedroom door. "Luka, you must get dressed quickly. We have to leave! We aren't safe here and we must go to your parents' house!" Luka did as he was told and they left the small cottage carrying only a small bag with a flask of water and a loaf of bread.

Luka and his grandad ran along the rugged terrain and arrived at the house fairly quickly but they could hear gunshots. As they got closer they saw soldiers marching up towards the cluster of humble homes. Tension filled the air and suddenly shots rang out, shattering the air and sending birds flying off from the trees in anguish.

"Run to the house!" cried Luka's grandad. But no sooner had he said it, somehow, Luka had no idea how or who, but his grandad had been shot in the crossfire and he fell to the ground.

Luka's father came running out of the house followed by his little sister, Jasmine and his mother. "Are you all right? Are you hurt?" His father asked, eyes alight with concern. Luka shook his head, tears streaming down his face. There was another explosion and the smoke grew thicker with each passing second and they could see soldiers drawing closer from the distance.

Luka clung onto his parents, tears streaming down his face as they ran towards safety. Amidst the chaos and destruction around them, the remnants of a meaningless conflict that had led to the death of his grandfather and their family home burned to the ground. Luka knew that he would remember this moment for the rest of his life.

Luka and his family fled to a hotel in Zadar to become refugees together with thousands of other Croatians. He didn't really understand what was happening around him. He saw his parents were worried and they were all deeply upset at having lost his grandfather and his home. Little Luka and his sister Jasmina had to deal with the sound of grenades and gunfire every day. They also had to avoid landmines that might be buried around the perimeter of the hotel and there was no electricity or running water. One day his dad came up to their room with something hidden behind his back. He came over to Luka and surprised him with a rugged and tatty football that had seen better days.

"Hey, I found this for you today. I thought we could play together," his dad said with a big grin. Luka leaped up from

the bed hugging the football tightly.

"Thanks Dad!" he replied. That football served as a beacon of hope in Luka's existence, as he wished that one day he would be able to escape his war-torn life. As the days dragged on in the refugee camp, Luka found solace in his football. He ran along the corridors, played in the hotel car park and he even took it to bed with him!

A twist in fate revealed that the owner of the hotel, Tomislav Basic, was also one of the directors at NK Zadar football team. He spotted Luka playing against the hotel wall in the car park one day and decided to approach him.

"Hey kid, would you like to come play football for our team?" Luka's heart raced with excitement.

"Yes, I would love to!" he replied, eagerly. The promise of football gave Luka two years of shimmering hope amidst the sound of his country at war. But then the shimmer turned to shame when the coach came to talk to him one day after training.

"Sorry son, you just don't have the build for this sport." Luka heard the words echoing again and again in his mind. "We're going to have to let you go, but maybe if you get stronger one day…" His words trailed off and the rest became a blur to Luka.

As he returned to the hotel with the rest of the refugees, Luka suddenly remembered a story about knights and dragons that his grandad had read to him. A young knight named Elaro had embarked on a quest to prove his bravery when he faced an ancient dragon. Elaro discovered that true strength comes from within and that with courage and determination, any obstacle could be overcome. Luka thought about those cosy reading sessions with his grandad and decided that he wanted to make him proud. I want to be a professional footballer and nothing is going to stop me!

And Luka pushed all the way with pure perseverance. From sunrise to sunset, he kicked, dribbled, and practised tirelessly, fuelled by his determination to make a mark in the world. At 16 he was signed for Dinamo Zagreb, Croatia's biggest club which was key in paving the road to his future success. He was initially loaned out regularly but Luka refused to give up, stopping at nothing as he knew that his big break was going to come. It was through these loans that he was able to prove that the quality of his game spoke for itself and he truly began to shine. Nobody spoke about his physique anymore and he was given a key role in the Under-21 team at international level.

Luka Modrić made his full Croatia debut in March 2006 against Argentina and the football prodigy, Messi! As his team stood in line, arms linked and listened to the Croatia anthem, his heart swelled with pride. I'm going to show the world that I'm one of the best midfielders in history!

The whistle blew and play began. Argentina was playing strong, top form defending and they were dominating the game with possession. They scored a goal and the Croatians knew they had to up their game to even the score. But the Argentinians scored again and the roar of the crowd echoed through the stadium, vibrating with a mixture of excitement and tension. It was half-time, and with the team trailing by two goals, Luka gathered his team-mates in the locker room. As usual his voice was quiet, calm and steady.

"Listen up. I know things haven't gone our way in the first half. But remember why we're here. We didn't come this far to give up now."

The team looked each other in the eyes, rose from their seats, and with a renewed sense of determination they stepped back onto the field. Luka's words echoed in their minds and they were ready to fight for the match. Seventeen minutes into the second half Luka dribbled forward on the left and made a run into the danger zone. He made a perfect cross, jumped two defenders and headed the ball down into the bottom corner.

Gooooooooooooaaaaaaaaaaaaaaaaaal! The fans went wild and Luka ran to his team sliding along the grass on his knees. The fans were on their feet now, chanting his name. Luka got up and kept his cool. He knew that they still had work to do.

There were only nine minutes left on the clock and a little stoppage time. At the corner-kick, Luka was up against

Messi who was a bit smaller than him. Luka knew there was only going to be one winner and leapt high, steering the ball into the top corner. 3-2 to Croatia!

Luka punched the air and he realised that his big break had come. He wasn't just dreaming big any more, he was playing big!

Luka knew that he had made the definitive leap to the elite when Tottenham Hotspur paid €20 million for him. He played there for four years before he was signed by Real Madrid for a whopping €30 million! And still today, Luka Modrić continues to play for the Spanish team where he is viewed as a true football legend.

Modrić is known all over the world for his humility, professionalism, and enormous dedication to the sport. His journey from humble beginnings in Zadar to becoming one of the most celebrated players in football serves as an inspiration to aspiring athletes worldwide.

FACTS AND CAREER HIGHLIGHTS

- Luka Modrić has won five Champions Leagues, three La Ligas, four Spanish Super Cups, four European Super Cups and one Copa del Rey.
- In 2018 Modrić led Croatia to the World Cup. Despite their defeat, losing to France in the final, the country celebrated a historical second place.
- Modrić won the Ballon d'Or in 2018.
- Between 2007 and 2022, the midfield maestro has been awarded the Croatian Footballer of the Year award a record 11 times!
- Having played at the 2006, 2014, 2018 and 2022 World Cups, as well as the 2008, 2012, 2016 and 2020 European Championships, Modrić became the first player to appear at both the Euros and World Cup in three different decades, a testament to his longevity at the highest level.
- Modrić's first pair of shin pads, which he used in the Bosnian League before ultimately giving them away, featured a picture of the Brazilian Ronaldo.
- Modrić has a lifetime sponsorship deal with Nike for football boots and apparel. He has featured in their commercials alongside Cristiano Ronaldo.
- Modrić is a philanthropist. He donated his 2022 World Cup-worn jersey to earthquake victims in Turkey and he has also helped to fund the hospital in his hometown, Zadar. He also supports numerous charities to support

young refugees displaced by wars, orphanages, child malnutrition and various children's charities and hospitals.

> **The more difficult the victory, the greater the happiness in winning.**
> **PELÉ**

MARCUS RASHFORD

Marcus lifted his gaze from his laptop where he was working on his latest book and looked around the kitchen. The creamy-coloured leather sofa contrasted perfectly with its grey walls and wooden floors. Through the glass door of his fridge, Marcus looked at the cans of Coca-Cola lined up invitingly for when his friends came round. The scent of garlic-infused spaghetti bolognese still hung in the air. It was his favourite dish as a young boy, and today Marcus had cooked it himself. He had become an avid chef since recently learning how to cook - quite an achievement considering that previously he didn't even know how to peel a carrot!

Marcus breathed in the smell again. Wow! That smells so good! His mind wandered back to when he used to go with his mum and his four brothers and sisters to the soup kitchen. They often didn't have enough money to eat so they had to

rely on school lunches, food banks and soup rooms. On that particular day there were huge containers of food, casseroles, salads, and watermelons all lined up along a shiny metal work surface. Marcus goggled at the sight of the watermelon. They didn't get to eat much fresh fruit because it was expensive.

"Only serve one slice per person," the volunteers were told by the friendly lady in charge as she poured dressing over the great bowls of salad and peeled plastic wrap from the casserole dishes. Marcus caught sight of a teenage girl in front of him in the line.

"Could I have a salad, please?" she asked. The friendly lady brought her a plate of greens with fresh fruit and nuts. The girl's eyes grew wide. "These are the first fresh vegetables I've had in four months," she exclaimed.

Marcus was so hungry that his mouth started to water but he was never one to complain. He distracted himself by looking around. He looked at the people's faces. They all sat at long tables eating, some happy and some sad. Some chatting excitedly with friends and some eating alone in the corner but each with a story to tell.

"Come and stand here. We're next." Marcus' mum Melanie jolted her little boy back from his distraction and lined up her five children to keep their place in the lengthy line. "Give them all a scoop of everything please," she said. Marcus and his siblings held their trays obediently and took their food to sit down. Melanie brought her tray of food to the table and started to share out her serving onto the trays of her five children. That was what she did on most days during the holidays as she knew that her children hadn't had a good school lunch put inside their tummies. Melanie knew that five growing children needed food more than she did and often sacrificed her own dinner so that her children got a decent amount to eat.

The night before had been tough as they'd missed the bus to go to the food bank. Melanie was trying to make some dinner with the few ingredients that she had. They didn't even have a loaf of bread in the house, but rice saved the day, although there wasn't much of it. They all sat down together and the children tucked in, starving as they always were.

"Where's yours, mum?" asked Marcus.

"I've already eaten mine, thanks love," she lied. She knew that if her children found out she hadn't eaten, they would insist on giving her some of theirs. That night, the rice had been all Marcus had eaten in the entire day because it wasn't term time at school so he hadn't had his usual school lunch. As soon as dinner was over, Marcus went to bed, forcing himself to go to sleep so that he would stop feeling the pangs of hunger.

Marcus was jolted back to the reality of his kitchen and his laptop as he heard a crash of lightning outside his house.

He looked over at his girlfriend, Lucia, sitting at the breakfast bar on one of the stools. "I need to stretch my legs," he said. Lucia looked out of the window,

"Well, you'll have to make do with a walk around the house because it looks like the rain is here for the day." Marcus walked to the hallway where he had cleverly created a built-in, glass trophy cabinet under the stairs. It contained football memorabilia that he had collected since his official first-team debut with Manchester United in 2016.

The trophies, the England caps, the medals… every item had a story to tell. Marcus had come a long way from a childhood that had been no fairytale.

Marcus looked at his gleaming, polished trophies. A reminder of the huge turning point in his life that came when he was 11 years old and he became the youngest boy selected for Manchester United's Schoolboy Scholars scheme. He had worked hard at school and proved he had a talent for mathematics. His scholarship led to an excellent education at secondary school and Marcus left school with an impressive total of nine GCSEs, balancing the rigours of his education with the demands of football. Marcus then pursued a National Diploma in Sports.

He continued to gaze at his shiny silverware that stood so proudly in the cabinet under the stairs. He thought back to the match that had made him who he was today. The Europa League, Old Trafford Stadium and 18-year-old Marcus was in the starting line for his first-team debut. The commentator was buzzing with expectation.

"He's a big strong lad, and as fast as lightning. I wouldn't be surprised if he scored tonight."

Marcus looked around the stadium, feeling the electric atmosphere as fans eagerly awaited the start of the game. The air was filled with chants: "Hello, hello, we are the Busby boys!" Fans were waving flags, and holding up banners to show their support. Marcus felt the anticipation building up inside him and as play began, the crowd erupted into a deafening roar.

And the commentator was on fire. "Here comes Rashford, belting it down on the right. And he's passed a perfect ball to Mata, and it's a give-and-go. He's got it. And it's a goal! Marcus Rashford, Manchester born and bred. The stuff that dreams are made of!" Marcus ran over to the Family Stand set in the crowd and celebrated the goal with Dean Henderson. He felt like he could fly. Marcus was experiencing one of the greatest feelings in the world.

Less than 12 minutes passed and Marcus had the ball again. Was Old Trafford going to see this new, up and coming star score another goal? Apparently not, as a tackle came from the left and he'd lost possession. The match appeared to hit a lull and the stadium was quiet, but then suddenly sprung to life just short of the half-hour. The commentator boomed again: "And it's a cross by Guillermo Varela that has fallen kindly for Rashford who's just inside the area. I think we could have another goal here. And we do. And we do! Rashford has just lashed a second goal into the top corner on his Premier League debut."

Marcus remembered the match like it was yesterday. He knew that even if he didn't earn all the money that he did playing football, and even if he wasn't famous, he would still play because there is nothing else like it. Football was his life and he felt so lucky to be able to play it. He felt so blessed thinking back to the life of poverty that he had come from and he felt driven to help others who lived in the same poor conditions that he knew only too well. That is one of the most heart-warming things about Marcus Rashford - his desire to give back and help others.

Marcus's own experience of growing up in poverty has ignited his desire to do more than just tackle on the football pitch. Now, he tackles the issues of child poverty, racism, and homelessness across England. Marcus says he believes that having grown up with his own struggles and pain, his hardships have grown into the main cause of his drive and motivation to help others today. He is a high profile footballer who could be spending his time focusing exclusively on sport and looking after himself, but instead he spends a lot of his spare time volunteering and campaigning for a better life for others. This is remarkable and it is no wonder that he is one of the best role models that youngsters should look up to today.

FACTS AND CAREER HIGHLIGHTS

- Rashford has won five trophies for his club and country so far in his career - all with Manchester United.
- This world class striker has scored in 10 consecutive Tmatches for Manchester United at Old Trafford, a record that he jointly holds with club legend Dennis Viollet.
- Rashford's idols while growing up were Wayne Rooney and Cristiano Ronaldo.
- He has written and published several books and launched a book club to promote reading and literacy among children.
- In 2019, he helped create the 'In the Box' campaign - an initiative to supply homeless people with much-needed essentials over the Christmas period. Showing his dedication to the cause, both he and his mother attended shelters over winter to help distribute the boxes.
- In 2020, Rashford launched a campaign to extend the government's free school meal initiative for children from low-income families during the summer months.
- In recognition of his charitable efforts, Rashford was awarded an MBE and was named as one of Time Magazine's 100 most influential people in the world.

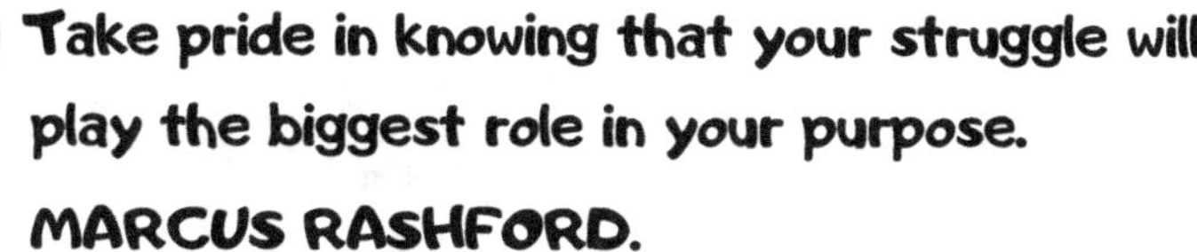

Take pride in knowing that your struggle will play the biggest role in your purpose.
MARCUS RASHFORD.

114

RICARDO KAKÁ

One by one, the team walked through the long, dim tunnel, and out into the bright lights of the stadium. They were greeted by an eruption of cheers and a spectacle of colour. Ricardo Kaká looked around the stands and felt enormous pride in being captain of the Sao Paulo junior team. They were about to play the final of the Juvenile Champions Cup.

The team had been on top form throughout the tournament and all they needed now was one more win to go home with the ultimate prize in junior football. The referee blew the whistle and while the fans made as much noise as possible, play began. In the 18th minute, Raul passed the ball to Ricardo. He turned quickly and it was a foul! He fell hard but got quickly back up to his feet for a free kick. As he got up he realised that they had an opportunity for a goal. He tried to stay calm, looked over to Maximiliano who was

already waiting and he curled the ball into the six-yard box with calculated precision. Maxi's right foot came back, pelting the ball into the back of the net leaving the goalkeeper without a chance. What a goal! What an assist!

São Paulo's players had come onto the pitch full of confidence but after the goal they were on fire. They were dominating the game with the majority of possession. In the second half, Ricardo had the ball at his feet and he was showing off his strong midfielder skills as he dribbled as fast as lightning, passing defenders with ease and he was one-on-one with the goalkeeper. Should he aim for bottom left or bottom right? No, he was going to take a risk and go top corner. Ricardo kicked the ball and it went up, hurling towards the goal. Is that going too high? I think I've misjudged it! But no, the ball started to drop and went flying into the top right corner without an inch to spare.

Gooooooooooooaaaaaaaaal!

They sailed through the remaining part of the match and it seemed like it was over in minutes. When the full-time whistle blew, Ricardo sprinted over to his team-mates and they all ran around the pitch hugging each other. What a feeling!

"We did it!" he said to Raul. "We're taking the São Paulo cup home!"

They could hear the fans in raptures throughout the stands, cheering and waving flags and scarves. Ricardo looked over to his mum and dad standing in the family box, hands in the air and cheering frantically. He was so grateful for all the support that they had given him; a privileged childhood, never in need of anything. And here they were again today, offering their unfaltering support.

Ricado went on to make his professional debut shortly after the triumphant victory of the Juvenile Champions Cup. Two months into this next step in his career, Ricardo and his team had made it through to the second leg of the final in the Rio São Paulo tournament. They were 1-0 down but within a few minutes everything would change. First, Ricardo side-footed an equaliser and then less than two minutes later he shimmied past the defender on the edge of the box and slid a winner inside the goalposts. Two goals in two minutes changed Ricardo Kaká's life.

After that match, he became the epitome of football stardom.

Suddenly his world was altered and everyone recognised him on the street. His rise to the top of football had begun.

Only a few days had passed since the match and wherever Ricardo went, he was followed by journalists, all posing the same question: "What does it feel like to be one of the future stars of Brazilian football, Kaká?" But Ricardo was humble and he always laughed off such compliments. He wasn't only talked about in Brazil. Clubs across the world had their eye on the new football prodigy and offers began to flood in from European clubs wanting Kaká on their team. German club Bayer Leverkusen made an offer for Ricardo but São Paulo turned it down saying they wanted more money for him.

Ricardo was disappointed as he had been keen on the idea of the transfer to the German team. He decided to go and visit his grandparents in Caldas Novas to have some time out and relax after the downer.

He was lying by the pool and it was a sweltering day.

"Do you want some fresh lemonade?" his grandfather called from the kitchen window. Ricardo looked up from the sunbed.

"I'd love some. Thanks."

Ricardo's grandfather came out to join his grandson, carrying a jug of iced lemonade and two tall glasses. As his grandfather poured the lemonade he asked, "So how are you feeling?" Ricardo looked up from his glass and smiled.

"I'm good, grandad. I was disappointed not to go to Bayer, but hey, I have a professional contract with São Paulo and I'm going to play football to the highest level possible!" Ricardo wiped the sweat from his brow. "Gosh it's hot today. I need to cool off in the pool before I melt."

Ricardo got up and went over to the diving board at the end of the pool. Beaming from ear to ear, he looked over to his grandfather, feeling the rays of the sun beating down on the back of his neck. He bent his knees and leaped from the board, diving into the crystal clear water. The impact was sudden, the pain was excruciating. Ricardo felt the blow to his head as it collided with the swimming pool floor. He came up to the surface, disoriented, and he could hear his grandfather saying something but didn't know how to respond.

Everything went blank.

At the hospital there was initially an extremely bleak prognosis from doctors. Ricardo had fractured his spine and the injury initially appeared to be incredibly serious, to the point that they feared Ricardo may be paralysed for the rest of his life.

"You mean I may never be able to walk again?" asked Ricardo. The chief doctor took a step closer.

"No, Ricardo, we can now confirm that our initial fears are not warranted and the injury will not lead to paralysis." Ricardo closed his eyes as they welled up with tears of relief. "But," the doctor continued, "you may not be able to ever return to normal activity and we will have to wait to see how your vertebrae heal and how your recovery develops." Ricardo opened his eyes again and his head began to reel. Never return to normal activity? My normal activity is professional football. God help me!

Ricardo did indeed spend a lot of time in that hospital bed praying to God.

His prayers were miraculously answered because Ricardo was back on his feet in record time from such a grave injury.

Not long after he was able to return home but it wasn't plain sailing from there as the doctors explained that just because he could walk again, did not mean that he would be able to return to football.

Ricardo refused to give up on his dream though and he confronted the challenging road to recovery. Days turned into weeks as he pushed himself through the agony of physical therapy. He was committed to persevere and regain strength in his legs.

Ricardo attended his therapy sessions every single day without fail, diligently carrying out every single exercise that he was asked to do. Each small victory helped Ricardo to further ignite his determination to make a full recovery.

As unbelievable as it seemed to the doctors and everyone who knew of Ricardo's accident, he did make a full recovery and emerged stronger than ever. He returned to full form so quickly that people felt that a miracle had happened. Ricardo was able to recover without much damage and he was seen on the pitch playing next season.

He went on to play for São Paulo again and then later caught the eye of one of Milan's scouts. They were so impressed by the young Brazilian's skill and vision on the pitch that they signed him for an impressive €8.6 million. He started with a bang, even with all the elite players on the squad at the time. As a newcomer he scored 10 goals in 30 appearances and helped the club to win the Scudetto and the UEFA Super Cup. Ricardo himself was so grateful for such victories so shortly after his accident. He believed that his prayers had truly been answered, he had been blessed with a miracle. In gratitude he began to wear a shirt with an 'I belong to Jesus' slogan and he began to celebrate goals by pointing to the sky in gratitude.

Ricardo Kaká has been an inspiration to millions of people across the world. His journey from a potentially career-ending injury to becoming one of the football world's greats serves as a powerful reminder that setbacks can serve as stepping stones to success.

Ricardo Kaká refused to give up and let his injury define him. He defied the odds and came out stronger than ever. His legacy continues today as he inspires future generations and his influence extends far beyond the realms of a celebrity footballer. He is the essence of a remarkable individual.

I like that people can be big stars and still be humble.

OWEN HARGREAVES

FACTS AND CAREER HIGHLIGHTS

- Kaká was sold to Real Madrid by Milan for €70 million.
- He won the FIFA Player of the Year award twice, in 2007 and 2009. Kaká was instrumental in Brazil winning the World Cup in He is one of only four Brazilians to win the ballon d'Or alongside Ronaldo, Rivaldo and Ronaldinho.
- Since 2004 he has served as an ambassador against hunger for the UN World Food Programme hoping to inspire hungry children to believe that they can overcome the odds and lead a normal life.
- He launched the 'Kaká's Bosco' foundation, which focuses on improving the lives of underprivileged children through education and access to sports.
- He has millions of followers on social media where he remains connected to his fans and continues to inspire them with his posts and updates.
- Ricardo Kaká is married to his childhood sweetheart Caroline, and they have two children, Luca and Isabella.
- He retired in 2017 and lives with his wife and children in Orlando, Florida.
- Kaká is an avid reader but in recent years he has developed a passion for running marathons.

CONCLUSION

As the final whistle blows on the stories of these 13 remarkable individuals, they will continue to stand tall as beacons of hope and inspiration for aspiring athletes worldwide. Each player in this collection of stories faced unique challenges - from poverty and discrimination to career-threatening injuries and personal tragedies. Yet, instead of letting these obstacles define them, they used them as fuel to ignite their passion for the game. With grit, determination, resilience, and unwavering hard work, they transformed their hardships into stepping stones toward their own legacies.

Their stories inspire millions around the globe, reminding us that success is not merely about talent but about perseverance in the face of adversity. As they lifted trophies, broke records, and won the hearts of fans with their incredible performances, they demonstrated that with dedication and belief in oneself, anything is possible. They remind us that success is not always easy or guaranteed, but it is always within reach for those willing to put in the effort and stay committed to their goals.

These footballers stand as a testament to the power of resilience and hard work in achieving our dreams. Their journeys exemplify the true essence of sportsmanship - pushing boundaries, overcoming setbacks, and rising stronger each time. Their stories remind us that greatness is not just measured by

trophies and accolades but by the sheer willpower to never give up when faced with challenges. They exemplify the power of perseverance, dedication, and passion for the beautiful game. In a world where challenges are inevitable, these 13 legendary footballers serve as inspiration for all who dare to dream.

You have to fight to reach your dream. You have to sacrifice and work hard for it.

LIONEL MESSI

www.ingramcontent.com/pod-product-compliance
Lightning Source LLC
LaVergne TN
LVHW041324200726
843509LV00009B/601